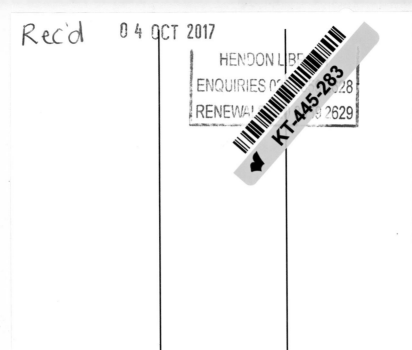

Please return/renew this item by the
last date shown to avoid a charge.
Books may also be renewed by phone
and Internet. May not be renewed if
required by another reader.

www.libraries.barnet.gov.uk

BARNET
LONDON BOROUGH

First published in Great Britain
in 2017 by Wren & Rook
Text © Hannah Witton, 2017
All rights reserved.
ISBN: 978 1 5263 6003 8
10 9 8 7 6 5 4 3 2 1

Wren & Rook
An imprint of Hachette Children's Group
Part of Hodder & Stoughton
Carmelite House
50 Victoria Embankment
London EC4Y 0DZ
An Hachette UK Company
www.hachette.co.uk
www.hachettechildrens.co.uk

Printed in England

MIX
Paper from
responsible sources
FSC® C104740

Publishing Director: Debbie Foy
Commissioning Editor: Elizabeth Brent
Consultant: Laura Hamzic

Designed & illustrated by Mélanie Johnsson
Cover design by Anna Morrison

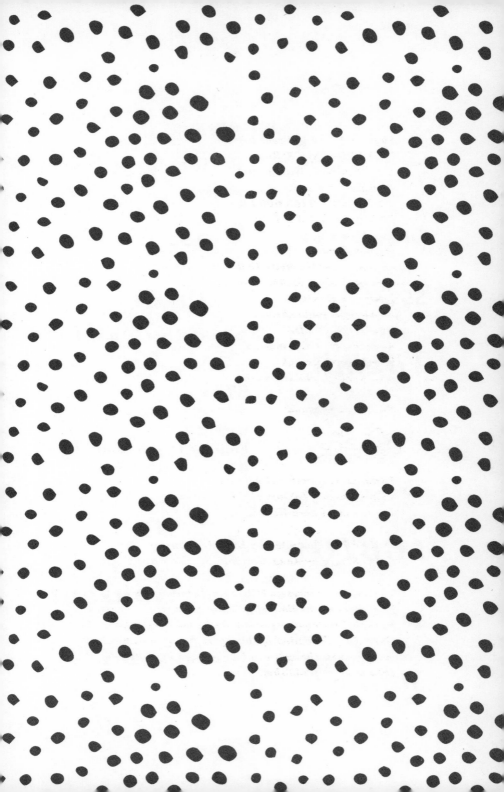

Contents

e you so
h please th
you like it o
I miss you
you to th
and back
to me mou
nk about ye
ryday pleas
me you got
chocolates

Doing it

introduction

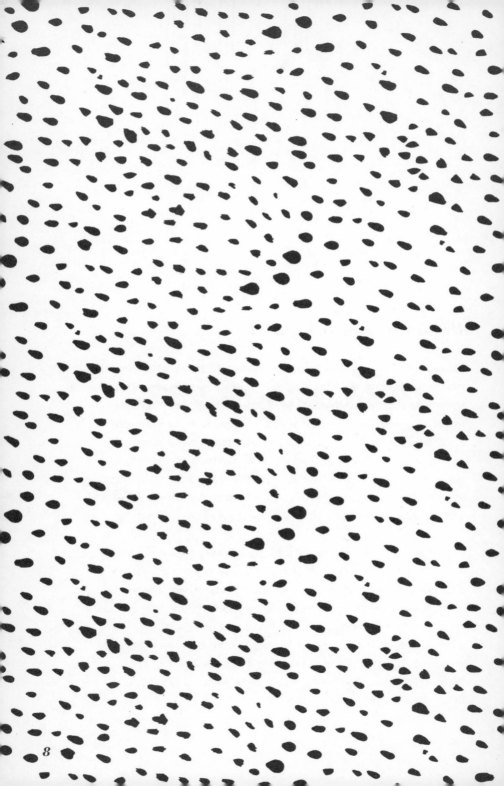

8

Hello there dear reader!

Thanks for picking up this book. I'm Hannah Witton and I'm a writer, vlogger and online sex educator. Sex and relationships education is something that I've been interested in for a while; some might say I have an unhealthy obsession with it. I argued with my RE teacher at school about it; I studied history at university but still managed to take all the sex modules; I wrote my dissertation on Victorian sex manuals; my whole YouTube channel is about sex and relationships, and I co-created a book club podcast where each month we read and discuss a book about sex. Does that make me obsessed? Maybe.

Let's start from the beginning. I grew up in a very open household when it came to the sex stuff. So much so that my family developed a bit of a reputation amongst my school friends. When I was about 13 years old, I invited a friend of mine over to my house after school for dinner. Another friend, who had previously had the privilege of dining at the Witton household, forewarned this newcomer, saying, 'Careful, they like to talk about vaginas and periods at the dinner table!' So it seems that talking about taboo subjects is something that I was raised by my parents to do.

In school and at home I had a decent sex education. I didn't think I was dying when I got my period for the first time, I knew how not to get pregnant (and how to get pregnant when the time finally arises – Grandma please stop asking), I knew that gay people were normal, and how to say 'no' if I wanted to. When I was 16, I went to a religious sixth-form college and during one of our weekly RE classes we were taught about healthy relationships. It was almost a sex-ed class, but I felt like something was missing, so I raised my hand,

'Miss? When are you going to teach us about contraception?' Valid question, I think.

But she said that she couldn't teach it because it wasn't in line with the religious teachings of the school. I couldn't get my head around this. Yes, I knew that some religions had rules against certain things, but I never thought it would make a difference to my education. The argument got a little heated, until I basically yelled, 'Look Miss, we're all 16/17, we're all having sex, so you could at least teach us how to do it safely!' The answer was still no. (Also, I know that not all 16/17 year olds are having sex, and that's completely fine, I was just trying to make a dramatic point.) But that was the first time I realised that something was wrong, and that we, as young people, weren't getting all the information we needed. And even though it was years later that I started making SRE (sex and relationships education) videos on YouTube, I feel like that experience must have stuck with me.

I uploaded my first video to YouTube in April 2011, and nine months later I uploaded my first sex education video. At the time I had a lovely audience of a few hundred people watching, and I noticed that they were mostly young women. I felt this need to be useful, to offer advice, to help them in some way, and I figured the best way for me to do this was to talk about sex. I knew that it was something not many people felt comfortable talking about, but I did for some reason, and so that seemed like the most obvious place to start. Six years later, I have made more than 50 videos talking about sex and relationships and now I'm writing a book about it!

I want this book to educate you, I want this book to feel like your friend gossiping with you, I want this book to make you feel normal, comfortable, empowered and in control of your body. I want this book to cradle and support you and I want it to allow you to just be yourself. Maybe I'm asking a lot from it, so I hope you understand that some of this has to come from you too.

Sex and relationships education is still not on the national curriculum in the UK. It's a dream of mine not only that the government changes this, but also that I can advise on what should be on the curriculum and maybe even teach some of it ...

Genuinely, I would love that! However, until then, you have this book. Here, you will find information, advice and support on everything ranging from puberty to porn, from consent to contraception, from masturbation to menstruation, from bisexuality to body image, from virginity to venereal disease (the old fashioned term for STIs, sorry, I just really wanted to continue the alliteration). There are also some personal stories in this book that I have never shared anywhere online before, along with advice, wisdom and a few anecdotes from friends of mine plus the occasional expert.

Officially this is a book is for anyone aged 14+ but if you're younger and feel like you're ready to read it then who am I to tell you otherwise? I hope there's something here for everyone, from teenagers figuring stuff out and experiencing things for the first time, to young adults still figuring stuff out and still experiencing things for the first time and the parents even still figuring ... you get it! We're all still working it out and experiencing new things. But in all seriousness, I hope you will find this book useful, insightful, and maybe even funny, whether you're 15 or 25.

Before we dive in, I should let you know that you don't have to read this book from cover to cover. It's not a story, there's no grand narrative and it can be read in any order.

So you can say, 'ooh I fancy a bit of healthy relationships today' and just read that section, or 'I'd quite like some porn today' and read that bit. That sounded weird, didn't it?

However, my point is it's completely up to you how you wish to consume this book: front to back; back to front; top to bottom (eh?!); just the sections you're interested in – the decision is yours.

I learnt a hell of a lot writing this book (I don't want to give anything away, but one thing involves a frog and some human urine ...) and I hope you learn some new things, too. I also just hope that you enjoy it. We touch on some heavy topics ... and yes, sometimes when we talk about sex and relationships we have to get serious, but there's an equal amount of importance placed on the fun and the pleasure of sex. Except maybe (spoiler alert) in the section on break-ups. As you will find out, that particular part became an interesting struggle to write.

At this point I also feel like I need to say if you are my parents, grandparents or related to me in any other way, thank you so much for supporting me and buying this book but please put it down right now. We don't want Christmas and Passover to be weird.

14

Chapter 1

healthy relationships

16

What does a healthy relationship look like?

I'm starting with this because if there's anything I want you to take away from this book, it's that you deserve and you are entitled to healthy relationships. Whether that's with your romantic or sexual partners, your friends, your family, your colleagues, your peers or, most importantly, yourself. A healthy relationship is the foundation for any kind of strong, successful bond between people. Whether you've known someone five years or five minutes, it's important, crucial even, that everyone is happy and everyone knows what's up.

Some crucial components of a healthy relationship ...

Trust

A relationship without trust is toxic. You need to trust your partner and your partner needs to trust you. Relationships can feel scary because you are essentially giving someone else your (metaphorical) heart and trusting that they won't mistreat it. If you don't trust your partner, you need to ask yourself why, and then talk to them about it. Jealousy and paranoia are the enemies of any healthy relationship – if the trust is there you won't feel anxious, jealous and on edge all the time. OK, sometimes at the beginning of a relationship you feel those emotions along with excitement, which is fine because you're at the 'will we/ won't we?' stage. But once you're further down the line and you're in a secure relationship, it should be just that – secure. Being in a trusting relationship means telling each other the truth and believing each other, keeping promises, having confidence in the other person and feeling safe with them physically and emotionally. It also means not worrying what your partner is up to when you're not around, and staying away from their phone and personal messages. Spying on someone is just not cool. Don't expect to trust someone fully straight away, either. Trust is something that you build together in a relationship and it's something you have to earn.

Respect (just a little bit, just a little bit)

Aretha Franklin knows exactly what's up. I'm not going to lie, 'respect' is one of those words that I use a lot, but I've never really thought much about what it actually means. So here's the dictionary definition: 'a feeling of deep admiration for someone or something elicited by their abilities, qualities, or achievements.' So I like to think of it as recognising how badass your partner is. I've never bought into the idea of 'finding your other half'; everyone is whole on their own and being in a relationship makes a team, not a single unit. Respecting your partner means recognising and valuing their independence. Respect their beliefs, their values, their life goals, their job, their hobbies, their friends and family. In a relationship it's not enough to just *have* respect for the other person, you need to show it, too. Whether that's giving them space to do their own thing, or actively supporting them in their career, or not trying to change them, you've got to show them a little R-E-S-P-E-C-T!

Communication

This is my favourite one. Can you have favourites when all of them are vital? I'm not sure, but I do know that I love talking and I love sharing. I'm working on the listening part, I promise. Communication might also be the hardest one because it's about opening up, allowing yourself to be vulnerable and giving someone the power to destroy you. OK, maybe 'destroy' isn't the best word, but opening up can be scary, especially if it's the first time you're bringing up a subject. However, if you already have the trust and respect then communicating will be much easier, and maybe even cathartic. Talk about what you need out of the relationship, what you want, what you expect, what you can give. Talk about boundaries and rules. Talk about jealousy (I think a small amount of jealousy is fine as long as you acknowledge it and tell the other person, 'Hey that made me feel a bit jealous'.) You know when you have that nagging thought in your head, something that is bothering you about a relationship, and just thinking about it frustrates you, doesn't fix anything and maybe even makes it worse? That's when you need to take some deep breaths and talk about how you're feeling. Easier said than done, I know, but I've never regretted telling someone what's on my mind.

And for those brief encounters, trust, respect and communication are equally important. Communicate your intentions and what you want to get out of it, and respect the other person's boundaries. Casual experiences should also be healthy and you shouldn't demand any less or accept bad treatment just because you're not in a relationship. Every person is unique so every relationship will be different in the type of communication you have, the level of trust, the amount of respect, your boundaries, your promises and rules. Having healthy relationships means making sure everyone is on the same page and happy.

Everyone wants to be in a power couple, right? Nope, just me? I want to be in a power couple and I want to be the best couple, the one that everyone thinks is 'relationship goals'. So I probably have unhealthy expectations for my relationships. But my superiority complex aside, to be a power couple, or just an amazing normal couple, you need a healthy relationship. You are not going to be able to achieve world domination ... I mean happiness and stability in your relationship, if you don't have trust, respect and good communication between you.

Not-so-healthy-relationships

At the other, most extreme, end of the healthy-relationship spectrum comes abusive relationships. And in the interest of balance, let's talk about those, too. First of all, if you are on the receiving end in an abusive relationship, it is not your fault. There is never an excuse for abuse. Whatever form it takes, it is not OK. Abuse is never OK. This is serious but it's important. An NSPCC survey of 1,500 UK teenagers showed that 25 per cent of girls and 18 per cent of boys had experienced physical violence from a partner, and 75 per cent of girls and 50 per cent of boys had experienced emotional violence from a partner. If we're lucky, we get taught what healthy relationships look like, but we're rarely taught what an unhealthy relationship looks like and how to spot early signs of abuse. A lot of little issues might not seem like a big deal at the time, but abuse escalates, and the small things can end up leading to more harmful or dangerous situations in the future. It's important to understand what is and isn't acceptable behaviour in relationships, how to spot the signs and what to do if you or someone you know is in an abusive relationship. When we talk about relationship abuse most people's thoughts jump to the extreme end of the spectrum – domestic violence. Yes, that is part of it, but abuse isn't always physical. It can include emotional abuse, sexual abuse, financial abuse, verbal abuse and controlling and manipulative behaviour. Here are some example of signs of abuse.

name calling

possessiveness

checking phone/emails

extreme jealousy or insecurity

explosive temper

pressuring to do things
you don't want to do

isolating you from your
friends and family

making you feel scared

making you feel down about yourself
and have low self-esteem

hurting you physically
or emotionally

pressuring or forcing you
to do sexual acts

Why checking your partner's phone is a type of relationship abuse

I made a video last year about relationship abuse and I got a lot of comments from people who were confused about why checking their partner's phone was abusive. So let's talk about that.

It comes down to trust, which as I said is absolutely crucial in any healthy relationship. Your text messages and your emails are your personal business. Just because you're in a relationship with someone doesn't mean you no longer have the right to your own private space. Remember, you're still you and it's okay to have some privacy in a relationship. In fact, it's healthy. Going through someone's phone without their permission is a sign that there is a lack of trust, and is very controlling behaviour. These days, a lot of our lives happen on our phones so it's more than just a gadget, it's a window into a person's life. Going through someone's phone can make them feel nervous or powerless, like they are being watched and monitored all the time, which is not how you should feel in a relationship. If you get an itchy feeling like you want to snoop on your partner's phone, think about why. Is it just out of curiosity or are you worried about their behaviour? Either way, don't do it.

Instead, talk openly with your partner about what is bothering you. If you don't find anything, you'll feel horribly guilty for looking through their phone and not trusting them. If you do find something then you're going to have to admit to looking in their phone without their permission. It's always best just to talk. If you think or know that your partner is checking your phone then firmly ask them to stop, and talk to them about why they are doing it. If they stop, that's great, but if they carry on then that should be a massive red flag. If someone doesn't respect your privacy, feels jealous and insecure and always wants to know what you're doing and who you're talking to, this could be an early sign of abuse.

What to do if you're in an abusive relationship

Remember it is not your fault. This is a horrible situation to be in, especially because the person abusing you is someone you are close to, and who is supposed to care about you. You might also be afraid of losing them. There is no way to sugar-coat this situation, it's awful, but knowing that you need to get out is the first step. Talk to someone you trust about what's going on – a friend, a family member, a professional or the police. No matter how isolated you have been made to feel, there are always people out there who care, and who will listen to and support you in any way they can. There are also loads of resources online, and more information about what to do and who to speak to at the end of this book.

What if your friend is in an abusive relationship?

This is such a difficult situation because if the abuser has made your friend feel isolated from everyone they know, they may take their abuser's side and not want to talk to you, which can be tough to witness. But you should let that person know that you will always be there for them and you're ready to listen whenever they want to talk. Encourage them to seek advice from someone with experience in helping people in abusive relationships, who will know what to do and how to support them.

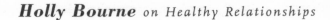

Holly Bourne on Healthy Relationships

It's important to start this by saying: I've always loved romance films. Adored them. I cried so hard at the end of *The Notebook* that my face actually had an allergic reaction to my own tears. I can recite every single sentence of *Pretty Woman* to you ('Big mistake, HUGE'). And the *Twilight* books saved me at a very dark time in my life called 'Jury Service'. But then I started working as a relationship advisor for a youth charity. I got trained to identify abusive relationships, and I couldn't help but notice how many relationship red flags are used in romantic movies as idealised plot devices. The more I watched romantic 'gestures' in films, the more I realised, if that gesture came up at work, I would be filling out a safeguarding form. I think one of the main problems is that actors in romantic movies tend to be very, very, very good looking. Or Ryan Gosling. Who is very, very, very, very good looking. And that detracts somewhat from all the problematic messaging. So, a useful mental imagery to have in your head is: would this still be sexy if Wormtail from Harry Potter was doing it? Here are just a few VERY WORRYING things that regularly happen in romance films:

The resist-kiss
It usually goes something like this. Girl goes to storm off. Guy grabs her back. Aggressively kisses her. She fights back for a moment ... and then dissolves into the kiss.

What's wrong with it?
Rape culture – in two short words for you. It buys into the myth that women are secretly always 'up for

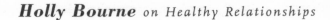

it', and it's just a matter of getting past their teasing pretences. A kiss like this is actually, legally, sexual assault. There is no clear consent here. You cannot read someone's sexual signals when they're storming away from you in a huff.

The Wormtail test:
You're having a massive go at Wormtail for being a traitor to Lily and James and then he JUST GRABS YOU AND KISSES YOU UNTIL YOU STOP FIGHTING.

The I'll-just-hang-here-outside-your-house
Either in the wooing stages, or the I-messed-up-and-want-you-back stages, there is a lot of hanging around outside the girl's house. Or watching her sleep. Or following her wherever she goes.

What's wrong with it?
Umm ... it's stalking. It really is stalking. And stalking is one of the most damaging and terrifying crimes you can commit against someone. It's also very misunderstood. Many people think it's something that only happens to celebrities, and that stalkers are weirdos in anoraks standing in the garden. But stalking is almost always done by an ex-partner, and can escalate very quickly into full-on violence.

The Wormtail test:
You wake up to find Wormtail salivating at the end of your bed, saying, 'I like watching you sleep.'

The If-I-Can't-Have-You-I'll-Die
Oh – isn't it romantic when someone hangs off a Ferris wheel until you agree to go out with them? Or the thought of life without you is so terrible that they try and get a parliament of vampires to murder them? Threatening to hurt yourself or kill yourself is the best way to prove your love, right? Riiiiight?

What's wrong with it?
This is actually a huge glaring warning sign of abuse in a relationship. It's manipulative, it's coercion, and you should never have to guilt someone into going out with/staying together with you. The words 'I cannot live without you' are not romantic and Romeo-esque. They're actually a huge alarm bell telling you to get out.

The Wormtail test:
Wormtail literally cuts off his hand to show his love for the Dark Lord. #JustSaying

The Dream-Denial
In almost all romance films there is a blow-up around 80/90 per cent of the way through. The lovers are ripped apart by a misunderstanding, preparing for the grand reunite at the end. However, usually during this separation, the female character really gets her sh*t together. She bags a dream job, or plans to move to a different city – one of her non-romantic dreams totally comes off. Only for her to get chased through an airport by her supposed love, telling her to 'WAIT' so she can give up her dream to make the relationship work.

What's wrong with it?
In a healthy relationship, you want your partner to succeed. You should not feel jealous or insecure about their ambitions. So it's rather damn worrying that so many male leads are perfectly happy with the idea of their soulmate giving everything up just for them.

The Wormtail test:
He's just chased you through an airport to stop you getting on an aeroplane and flying to your new

dream job. Would you give up said dream job for Mr Sexy-metal-magic-hand?

The You-Are-Not-Like-Other-Girls

There is something SPECIAL about this girl. The guy notices just how not like other girls she is. He tells her that she's better than her friends, better than everyone else. Isn't that nice of him? Isn't that a lovely compliment? I mean, love's about seeing the special in someone, isn't it?

What's wrong with it?

Let's just brush to one side the glaringly obvious fact that this much-used line is offensive to all girls everywhere. I mean, WOW. But anyway, again, this can be a warning sign of abusive behaviour. Abusers condition their victims into feeling special, different, and often talk down their friends and family. 'They're just not good for you' or 'You are better than them.' This very compliment can be used to isolate vulnerable people from their support networks. Always be wary of someone who tries to cut you off from the people you love.

The Wormtail test:

Wormtail and his cronies just LOVE wizards they deem more special than other wizards. So much so they call them Mudbloods. If Wormtail starts saying 'you're not like other witches' you're probably five minutes away from getting the Dark Mark tattooed on to your arm.

Holly Bourne is the bestselling author of *The Spinster Club* series. Her novel, *It Only Happens In The Movies*, explores the problematic nature of romance films and their impact on teenagers and their relationships.

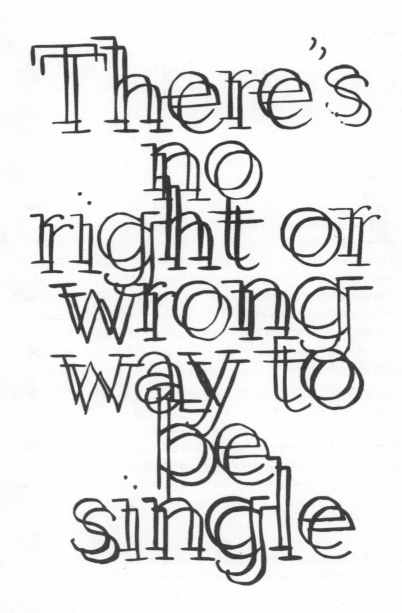

"There's no right or wrong way to be single"

Being single

I have mentioned several times online that I have been single for more than five years. Six years by the time this book comes out if I haven't found a boyfriend by then, but who's counting? My last serious relationship ended in 2011 when I was 19 years old. We had been going out for a year and a half, and had just gone long-distance because I'd moved to France, and long story short is I fell out of love and we broke up. The end. He's actually married now, which I found out via Facebook. Social media is a strange thing in the modern world of dating. You can find out so much about a person before you've ever really got to know them, and you are constantly reminded of people that you might much prefer forgetting for ever. An old fling from about four years ago recently got married and I couldn't help thinking, how many exes am I going to see on Facebook getting married? I'm 25 now, so the number is only going to exponentially increase until I'm 35, and all the divorces start coming in. (Sorry if you believe in true love, I'm a hopeless romantic too, but I'm also a realist and wear my cynicism like armour.)

I am a very fussy person and I seem to have a thing for American men. Even though I casually fancy a lot of people all of the time, I've only really properly fallen for three people during this single time. Two of them were American, and I know that it's possible because people have done it, but I did not succeed in nabbing myself a long-distance boyfriend either time. And I was heartbroken. Both of these men broke me. Which was a weird experience for my friends; they'd never seen me properly upset over a boy before and they didn't know what to do with me. But hey, it happens to the best of us. And the other person I fell for? Well, you'll soon see how that turned out.

There's no right or wrong way to be single. You can kiss as many people as you like, you can join every online dating site and app possible, you can pine over one crush for months, you can ignore all of this and focus all your energies on your family, friends, or career. Whatever suits you. When I'm single, my friends say they like to live vicariously through me (that'll give you an idea of my love life). Don't get me wrong, there are definitely times in my life when there are no boys in the picture at all, but they don't last very long. My friends often joke about having to take notes to keep up with who I fancy or who I'm dating. I like the drama and the excitement of constantly changing situations. Even though it can be stressful sometimes, it does mean I have a lot of great anecdotes ...

1 I once hid in a guy's kitchen when his parents came over one morning to pick up some stuff from his house. *I felt like a spy, it was pretty cool.*

2 I once went on a date with a guy that was the most uncomfortable thing ever, but I couldn't put my finger on why. It wasn't until afterwards, when I was talking about what happened to a friend, that I realised *he'd basically been using 'pick-up artist' moves on me.* Gross.

I did the absolutely clichéd thing of sleeping with a university friend at a friend's wedding a year after we graduated.

3

4

I have made two best friends out of different situations where we were *both involved with the same guy.*

I literally ran away from a guy who was trying to hit on me even though I'd already told him I wasn't interested. He chased after me and I ran into a kebab shop (this was at 3am in Brighton) and bumped into a girl *(Oshen, you legend!)* who had watched my videos, and a bunch of her friends. They stood by and made sure I was safe whilst I shouted at him for being a massive creep.

5

6

I slept with someone whose birthday is 14th February, and *he had a birthmark in the shape of a love heart on his penis.*

And those are just some of the more PG stories (except maybe that last one).

In my five years of singledom I feel like I have become an expert in the area, and so I want to share with you my wisdom. We've all seen the films depicting being single as just a transition period between relationships, which are the real deal. According to them, this (hopefully brief) time in our lives will consist of lots of crying, lots of partying, lots of sleeping with random strangers and lots of tragic dates in the desperate hunt to find a partner. And I don't relate to any of this at all (well, OK, maybe some of it). Some people are scared of being single, others expect it to be the best time of their lives, but this is what it's really like being single (for me anyway):

You don't have a 'somebody'

When you're invited to friends' parties or dinners and they say 'boyfriends/girlfriends/partners welcome', you just show up on your own. When there's a play, comedy show, music gig, art gallery, museum – any fun activity – that you really want to go to, instead of having your go-to person and always having a buddy to go with, you have to ask around all your friends to see who wants to go with you. This is tiresome and can get annoying if you're like me and you want to go to all the things. But the plus side is that you get to carefully select the best friends to go with, the ones who will appreciate it the most and be just as into it as you are.

If you disappeared, how long would it be until people noticed?

OK maybe this is a bit dark, but I think about it a lot. Most of my friends I see or speak to weekly, but not daily. And when I first moved to London I lived in a warehouse with 11 other people and no one ever noticed when I was gone for a few days. Now I live with two other people and I'm a lot more confident that someone would notice if I went missing. But if you're in a relationship and you have a person you speak to every day, you wouldn't even have to worry about this.

Not having to check in with anybody

I guess you could call this the plus side of it maybe taking a week for people to realise you've disappeared, but hey this is one of my favourite things about being single. It's also the thing that I've gotten most used to and I think will be the hardest for me to change about my habits. When you're single and you're not living with your parents you don't have to tell anyone what you're doing day-to-day. Maybe this is especially true for me because I'm freelance so I don't have a boss to check in with either. I can go to the cinema on a Wednesday morning and no one will know or be mad at me for going to see a film without them.

Couples happen in waves

One minute it'll feel like all your friends with partners are breaking up, and then a few months later all your single friends will be coupling off. Is this a thing? Is there any science behind this? I've no idea but it is a legit thing I've noticed.

You just need a snuggle

Forget sexual frustration – that can be dealt with. I majorly suffer with snuggle frustration. I have four pillows in my bed but I actually only sleep with one under my head. The others I use to put my arms and legs around. I tell people that it's because it's meant to be good for your back (which it is) but really I just desperately want a cuddle. Luckily, I've got lots of friends who will spoon me and stroke my hair but let's be real, it feels so good coming from a romantic/ sexual partner.

Sometimes you will just feel so damn lonely

Yes I am a strong, independent woman and I enjoy being single and I am single by choice. I date people, I fancy people, I sleep with people and for the most part it hasn't worked out, hence the single status. Most of the time I love this lifestyle and I don't feel like anything is missing at all. But then there's the odd day where everything stinks and you crave a relationship because you feel so alone. There's no point glossing over this and pretending that being single is amazing all the time, because it isn't. Sometimes (rarely though) I just really want a boyfriend. Sue me!

Your friends and family are your everything

This isn't meant to sound scary, it's actually wonderful! Relationships take up a lot of time and energy, and when you're single you have so much more of it to spend on your friends and family. For me personally, these are the people that have filled whatever void it is that I'm supposed to be feeling without a partner. I get all the love, acceptance, bonding, familiarity, sense of belonging, support and cuddles that I would get from any partner.

As you can see there are good things and bad things about being single, but that's also the case for relationships. Listen to yourself, what you want and what's good for you. Whether that's breaking up with someone because you need some time alone or jumping into a relationship because you're sick of being alone, think about why you want these things and if it's coming from a good place. Everyone needs different things at different times in their life so don't beat yourself up if you've not had a partner in a while (there's nothing wrong with you!). Being single doesn't make you unworthy of anyone's love. The way I like to think of it is that people have to prove to you if they're worthy of your love. You do you. Live your life the way that you want to and along the way you'll meet people trying to do the same thing. I genuinely believe it is good to have some single time in your life. It's so valuable, especially when you're young, because this is really the time you can put yourself first. No mortgage or kids, AM I RIGHT? You can explore the things that you want, and be a bit selfish for a while. There's nothing wrong with that (as long as you're not hurting other people!). I remember when I turned 20 I said to myself that this would be my hedonistic decade. That's not to say you can't be hedonistic when you're older, but I planned on making a conscious effort to seek out the pleasures in life in my 20s. And that doesn't just mean sex; it means food, self-indulgence, pampering, travel, looking after your body and wellbeing. When you're single you can put yourself first and you shouldn't take that for granted.

For me, as clichéd as it sounds, being single has allowed me to really figure out who I am. What makes me tick, why I behave a certain way in situations, what kind of partner is best for me, what core beliefs and values matter to me the most, and what motivates me. I am very comfortable being left alone for long periods of time and I am happy in my own company. I've discovered that I like myself, even love myself, and I want to treat myself well, do nice things for me and take myself out on dates. Heck, I'd even pull a Sue Sylvester and marry myself if I could. Best life partner I could ask for.

Crushes

Crushes are the worst. But they're also the best. Sometimes your crush likes you back and it's the best feeling in the world and other times they don't and it sucks and it hurts. But it's also a great way to learn that rejection isn't the end of the world. We all get rejected and the sooner we learn that it's OK afterwards, the easier it is in the future to approach people you fancy, ask people out on dates and make the first move. Believe me, the time that it does work makes up for all those rejections!

When I was in school, mostly inspired by *Angus, Thongs and Full Frontal Snogging*, my friends and I came up with our own kissing scale. This was mainly because we were too immature to actually use words to describe what we were getting up to so instead had to use a numbered code. My friend Lucy also came up with a crush scale with easy '100 per cent accurate' measurements to follow to explain how much you like someone. Kissing scales and crush scales aren't meant to be taken seriously. There's no prescribed order you're supposed to do things in and you can miss out steps if you want, but they are a lot of fun and Lucy's crush scale gave me endless amounts of joy (although the context is definitely for when you're a bit older and out of school). Also, I'm not sure why clothing and haircuts are so important to Lucy but I guess they can say certain things about a person.

Disclaimer: obviously this is completely stupid and by no means do your crushes have to follow this scale. I just find it very funny and I love hearing about other people's kissing scales and crush scales.

Level 1

I could kiss you in a club

Pleasant to look at
If I was drunk …
Non-offensive clothing

Level 6

Maybe I need you

I want to have intimate,
frequent sex with you
Don't mind if you
meet my parents
This could be unhealthy

Level 2

Sometimes you cross my mind

More than two things in common
Nice haircut
Reasonably attractive
Not a dumb f**k

Level 5

Fire in my loins

I would have sex
with you multiple times
You're my +1
I think about you. A lot
I wish you were here

Level 3

We should hang out

Potential to date
The idea of seeing you
naked does not repulse me
Knows how to dress
We can maintain a conversation
I'm conscious of my behaviour
around you

Level 4

My friends have Facebook-stalked you

I want to have
consensual sex with you
Your flaws are now defendable
'Fanny flutter' when I see you
Nice and good humoured

Break-ups

For some reason, when writing the plan for this book, I forgot to include a section on break-ups. But I have to write about them because, guess what, I just got dumped. Like just now. Well 12 hours ago technically. I woke up at 3 a.m. this morning to a text from a guy who I'd been dating for just over two months and who I really liked. We were exclusive and it felt like we were on the cusp of a good relationship. It was an essay text that was so vague and just said he didn't want to hurt me so he was ending things now. Devastated, I couldn't get back to sleep, so I messaged a bunch of my friends – some in America who I knew would be awake – and then tossed and turned all night. This morning I've cried so much and tried to get in touch with him but he's ignoring me. My housemates are away this weekend and I don't want to be alone so I've rallied together my friends and am making sure that I keep busy. And I'm channelling all of my energy into this book. To be honest, I've been single for so long that I wasn't expecting to be in a relationship whilst writing. I felt like a bit of a fraud writing the section on singledom in the present tense because I had someone and I didn't feel single any more. But hey, I guess the single life isn't done with me yet. I think I am currently going through the second stage of grief: anger. So I apologise if this chapter is especially bitter, but it's real and you know what, actually, I don't apologise for it. Let's do this.

How to deal with a break-up (this is for me more than anyone, I need to take my own advice)

Going through a break-up sucks, whether you are the dumper or the dumpee. It just sucks. Everything sucks. But it's not the end of the world, especially if you're young and you don't have any legal contracts (marriage, mortgage) or children between you. It's a lot less complicated, think of that as a blessing. If you didn't want to break up and you're still completely besotted with the other person, it hurts like hell. Believe me, I know, I'm hurting so much right now. Do whatever you can to make yourself feel better, distract yourself or just allow yourself to feel everything. For hours I wasn't crying and I was really confused as to why I hadn't shed a tear yet but then it hit me like a ton of bricks and I couldn't stop. And it felt so good. So cry if you want to cry, scream if you want to scream, write a book if you want to write a book. Talk to your friends and family, whoever you feel like you can open up to and share how you're feeling. These people love you dearly (unlike the person who just broke your heart) and will be there for you and support you in whatever way you need. Invite your friends over, do fun things with them, have sleepovers. If you're anything like me, then you'll know that you cannot be left alone after a break-up. Too vulnerable. Too fragile. Must always be within reaching distance of a friend's body to hug and someone to talk to and laugh with.

Once you've got your support network in place, the next thing you're going to want to do is figure out how to deal with your ex. I would recommend talking to them, face-to-face preferably, because meanings can get lost through text or on the phone. Pick a neutral place and just hash it out. Get everything that you want to say to that person off your chest and give them time and space to say everything they need to say. The best break-ups are the ones with good communication and closure, and they hurt less in the long run. But don't go in with the expectation that you will change their mind – you're only setting yourself up for more hurt. Do it if you feel like you need to talk to them. It's good to have a proper conversation with no screaming or shouting (crying is acceptable) about why you're breaking up, so you can understand and get some closure. If you are the one breaking up with someone, it is so important that you talk to the other person. If you're having doubts, if you're confused and unsure, then talk. Don't sit on these feelings without talking them through with your partner first. It's not fair to spring a break-up on them out of nowhere with no warning signs (I may be projecting here).

How to get over someone

This applies to break-ups but also to those times when you have a crush that you need to move on from for whatever reason (they live in a different country, they don't fancy you back, they already have a partner). Here is my one-step, foolproof guide to getting over someone:

BREAK ALL CONTACT
WITH THEM

Do not see them, do not speak to them, don't text or call them. Mute them on social media and don't stalk their profiles. You need a clean break to fully get over someone. Being reminded of them in any way will only make it harder for you. This doesn't mean you can't be friends in the future, if you want to be, but initially it's a good and healthy idea to give yourself some distance. Time is the best healer, as clichéd as it sounds. Maybe by the time I finish this book I'll be fine. I'll let you know.

If you are the person who did the dumping, you need to respect the wishes of the person who is hurting right now. If they want space, give it to them. If they need to talk things through, be there for them. Make it as easy for them as you can whilst also drawing your own boundaries and looking after yourself.

During a break-up, there's a clichéd thing that everyone will tell you, and being recently dumped has made me realise more than ever how true it is. Unless you are one of those people who meet their 'soulmate' at 16 and stay with them forever, most of us have relationships that end. You may have one super-long relationship that lasts until death do you part, but before that you'll have loads of other relationships that end. Most romantic/sexual relationships are temporary, but do you know what's long-lasting? Friendship. It's now been three days since I was DUMPED BY TEXT and I wouldn't have been able to get through this weekend if it wasn't for my friends. The people who will always be there, whether I want to excitedly giggle about a new person I've met or cry about someone who has just broken my heart. Friends are so important because they will love you through it all, especially in times of need. Break-ups are hard, and sometimes people turn to an ex-partner to console them through it. This is not healthy. Don't do this. That's what your friends are for, so invest in your friendships.

43

44

The One

Speaking of 'soulmates', I want to talk about the whole notion of 'The One', because I don't believe in it. I recently visited one of my friends from university at her family home and met her parents. They were in their twenties when they met, after three dates they were engaged, six months later they were married and they're still together now. I'm sorry, what!? I quizzed them about it for ages, asking why they got married instead of just continuing to date and they said, 'we just knew'. As a 25-year-old who's dated a lot I would love to know what it feels like 'to know'. But I guess it's a case of 'you know when you know'. This is what my friends kept telling me when I wasn't sure if I'd had an orgasm yet – 'you'll know when you have one'.

As a hopeless romantic who's addicted to the Hollywood happy ending, I can't wait to be swept off my feet, have a whirlwind romance and live happily ever after. But as someone who has experienced dating, love, and break-ups, I also appreciate that this is just unrealistic (unless you are my friend's parents). Love is great but there is not a 'One' out there for everybody. You are not a half-person waiting for your 'other half' to come along and 'complete you'. You are whole and you are complete, just you, and you did that all by yourself. Congratulations! Maybe you've had lots of relationships that haven't worked out, but that's fine. Just because those exes weren't 'The One' doesn't mean they were any less important, significant or worth experiencing. For me personally, I think I'm going to stop obsessing over the idea of finding 'The One' and just enjoy the ride. (Can you tell I've just been through a break-up?)

Cheating

Why people cheat

Every person will have a different definition of what 'cheating' is, and that's why it's important to talk to your partner about these things and the boundaries you set in your relationship. Is kissing OK? Is flirting OK? What about sexting? Massages? Can you watch porn? What if you're still active on dating websites?

A lot of people say there is no excuse for cheating, but that doesn't really help us get to the bottom of why people do it. There are many reasons why someone might cheat: out of boredom, the thrill of doing something forbidden, fear of commitment and intimacy, craving intimacy, feeling alive, needing a sense of autonomy over your life. In these situations, cheating can be prevented by open communication in the relationship. Cheating is a sign that something needs to change, whether that means the relationship ends or something changes within it.

Why it's not OK

Cheating is one of the most awful things you can do in a relationship, yet so many people do it and so many people suffer because of it. Which sucks. Cheating sucks. At its core, cheating is lying, cheating is a betrayal and cheating shows a complete lack of respect for your partner. No matter how much you are tempted, how lonely you feel in your relationship, how turned on you get by other people, how bad your relationship is, cheating is never the answer. Cheating doesn't solve problems, it creates them. Often it's a sign that there's something already wrong in the relationship, and if this is the case then you should talk to your partner about it. No matter the reason or excuse, cheating is never OK.

What to do if your partner cheats on you

If you've been cheated on (as well as that being extremely emotionally painful) you have to decide what to do. For some people it's easy: you dump their ass. But for others it's not as simple as that: you try to work it out and to build back trust in the relationship. There is no right or wrong way to respond to cheating, and every couple is different. No one can tell you what to do in this situation, but try asking yourself some questions. Do you want to stay in the relationship? Can you build trust again? Can you move on from it? If you were my friend I'd obviously tell you to get the hell out of that relationship – better to know sooner rather than later. Listen to your friends – but ultimately what you decide is up to you.

What to do if you've cheated on your partner

Most people say that if their partner has cheated on them, they wouldn't want them to lie about it. But most people also say that if they did cheat they probably would lie about it. My advice: don't lie. Your partner deserves to know the truth; if you care about them at all you will open up and be honest about what's happened. Basically, it's the right thing to do. Healthy relationships aren't built on lies, betrayal and secrets – as dramatic as that sounds, it's true. Own up to your mistakes, it's the first step in trying to rectify them and make things better.

To be honest, I've never cheated on anyone (although I have been tempted) and I've never been cheated on (to my knowledge) so I can't speak from experience about the complexities of the hows and the whys and the what-to-dos. But trust your gut, talk to your partner, talk to your friends and family and if you can help it – don't cheat.

Alternatives to monogamy

It's important to remember that just because a relationship isn't monogamous (exclusive), it doesn't mean it's not healthy. A lot of people are in open (non-exclusive) relationships or are polyamorous (have more than one partner) but this is not the same as cheating. Despite the common misconception, it is still possible to cheat in open relationships. Every couple is different and if you want to be in an open relationship, make sure you talk about your desires, expectations and boundaries. It's not for everyone, obviously, but for some people it works wonderfully.

However, also remember that you don't have to be in an open relationship if you don't want to. You should never be made to feel like you have to do something you're uncomfortable with. If you go along with an open relationship that you don't want or aren't comfortable with, it will probably lead to problems further down the line.

In society, monogamy is the norm, but other types of relationship are just as valid if that's what works for the people involved. I've always wondered if I'd be able to have an open relationship and I think, although the idea sounds cool, I don't know if I'd be able to hack it in reality. You do you, I say, and don't judge others for their choices.

S.F. *On Polyamory:*

*I decided to start living polyamorously just
over three years ago. I'd had a number of
monogamous relationships before that point,
but throughout all of them I had a nagging
doubt as to whether they were the right thing
for me. I loved each of my partners very
much but I was constantly struggling with the
fact that I wanted to be with other people
as well. I knew polyamory, to varying extents,
existed – being in more casual relationships,
being in an open relationship, being able to
see multiple people at the same time – and
after way too long worrying over what it
would mean for me, and what others would
think of me if I were to label myself that way,
I decided to try it.*

*Since then I have dated maybe 25 people.
Some of the relationships eventually didn't
work, others chose to enter more closed
relationships, but there are also some people
I saw right from the beginning who I still
see now. I'm in happy, long-term
relationships with them, they're just
polyamorous relationships.I feel the key
thing to being polyamorous is to be very
clear about what you're looking for from*

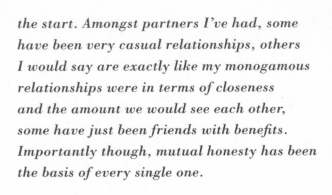

*the start. Amongst partners I've had, some
have been very casual relationships, others
I would say are exactly like my monogamous
relationships were in terms of closeness
and the amount we would see each other,
some have just been friends with benefits.
Importantly though, mutual honesty has been
the basis of every single one.*

*I happen to be pansexual as well as
polyamorous, meaning I am attracted to
people of all genders, but this doesn't have to
be the case. I know people of a whole variety
of sexualities who are polyamorous. I also
sometimes see more than one person as a
unit. I've dated a few couples and even a trio
of people but some polyamorous people prefer
to only see partners one on one. This is all
still under the umbrella of polyamory, which
just means to knowingly and consensually
engage in relationships with multiple people
and have your partners do the same.*

*When I tell people I'm polyamorous I get a lot
of reactions, but one of my least favourite is,
'I could never do that, I just love my partner
too much'. I understand that their sexuality
is different to mine. However I would really
stress, I don't feel I love my polyamorous
partners any less for the fact that I see more*

than one, just as I don't love my friends
any less for having more than one, or,
I imagine, a mother would love her many
children any less.

People also ask if I get jealous a lot. I don't.
Maybe it's just the way I'm made up, it's part
of my sexuality. The fact that someone I love
is with someone else they love and having a
great time? Good for them. Is there a lot of
stigma? Most people I have told have been
pretty good about it, if sometimes a little
ignorant. But then again, there are a lot
of people I don't feel I can tell. My family
definitely wouldn't understand, as they are
very traditional, and I don't tell people at
work either. I feel like they would understand
if I was gay and had a single partner of the
same gender, but dating multiple people? I
think that would be too odd for them.

Polyamory works for me right now. My
partners are great, and it gives me a freedom
to explore my sexuality I never felt like I had
when I was in monogamous relationships. But
my one wish would be that it was more widely
known, more widely understood and that I
could talk about it openly.

Chapter 2

virginity

How I lost my virginity

One night, when I was back in Manchester visiting my parents, we went out for dinner and this happened:

Hannah Witton ✓
@hannahwitton

Out for dinner with the parents & our waiter is my ex-bf from school who I lost my virginity to. Such a cliché of visiting your home town.

RETWEETS 61   LIKES 1,596

8:20 PM - 9 Jun 2016

I'm not a very nostalgic person but when it hits me, it fully knocks me out. After we graduated, my friends and I went back to visit our university, we went out and I cried on the dance floor at the silent disco to 'Let It Go' from *Frozen*. It was an emotional weekend, alright?

I don't think about losing my virginity that often. If I'm being brutally honest, it was a bit of a non-event. We were 16 and had been together for about six months, we'd spoken about having sex before, done 'everything else' and made sure we were ready. This to me meant waiting until after exams, because I was a massive nerd and didn't want sex to get in the way of my studies. No but really. Laugh all you want, I stick by 16-year-old-Hannah's decision. She knew what was best for her – smart. And he was totally cool with that. I actually almost lost my virginity on prom night. True story. Everyone knows that the best thing about prom is the after-party. Unfortunately for my squad and me it was a weeknight and no one had a free house and so, in our fancy dresses, heels and suits, we drank outside on a green (and yes this meant squatting and peeing in the street). We all slept over at my friend George's house and his sister wasn't home so my boyfriend and I got her room to ourselves. She's gay and I remember there being sexy pictures of ladies on her walls as we were making out and undressing each other. But when it came down to it I just couldn't. Each to their own – if you had sex for the first time on your prom night then congratulations, but it felt like such a cliché to me that it didn't sit right. So we didn't have sex then.

It actually happened in the most anti-climatic (no pun intended) way possible and that suited us perfectly. Exams were over and I was going to hang out with my friend Chris but beforehand I went to my boyfriend's house to say hi and chat. We did that but we also had sex. In the morning, on a mattress, on the floor surrounded by paint buckets and brushes in a half-decorated room. I even remember what underwear I was wearing – Primark girl boxers with red and white stripes if you were wondering. It didn't hurt; it was just uncomfortable. A strange and new sensation, this thing 'sex' that everyone talked about and said was so incredible and magic and life-changing. But there were no fireworks, there never are (unless you have sex on Bonfire Night). I didn't tell my friend Chris when we hung out later but I kept thinking, 'can he tell? Do I look different?' I expected this dramatic transformation from 'virgin' to 'not a virgin', from a girl to a woman, from innocence to experience, but that didn't happen. I was the same. My mum could tell though. She had given me the 'sex talk' a while earlier and we're very close so she knew it was going to happen but she didn't know when. Literally the day after, though, she turns to me in the kitchen and says 'so you're no longer a V then?' I was so embarrassed.

Even though it's not the most typically romantic story: no rose petals, no bubble bath or candles, I have no regrets about the first time I had sex.

We had a great relationship and we truly cared about each other, there was trust, respect and communication and I am so grateful for that because I know not everybody's experience is remembered so positively and fondly. It's also nice to know that eight years later we can still hang out and have a decent conversation without it being weird.

Don't have sex because you will get pregnant and die!

AKA virginity myth-busting

G rowing up we hear a lot of things about sex and virginity from family, friends, teachers and the media, so by the time it comes to having sex, we have all these worries and expectations about what's going to happen. At school, my sex education was simply 'don't do it until you're ready, and it's going to hurt.' I only recently started thinking about how messed up it is that we make young girls feel scared of sex before they're even sexually active. There's a lot of misinformation out there, but if we just talked about it openly and truthfully then there would be a lot less fear and shame surrounding sex. I want to bust some myths about virginity so we all feel more equipped with knowledge, and confident instead of scared.

What is 'real' sex?

The first thing I want to talk about is how we're taught that you lose your virginity the first time you have penetrative sex that involves a penis and a vagina. But by this standard there are loads of LGBTQ+ people who have technically never lost their virginity and aren't having 'real' sex, which is just plain wrong. There are so many different types of sex and the way we usually talk about virginity in society excludes the experiences of a lot of people. There's mutual masturbation, oral sex, anal sex, sex toys instead of penises ... There is no right or wrong way to have sex as long as all the people involved are consenting adults. It's by your standards whether or not you've had sex with someone, not anyone else's.

Does it hurt?

This is a question I hear all the time from young girls who are planning on having penetrative sex, and the answer is not necessarily. Sex can hurt, but by no means does your first time have to be painful. If you are relaxed and aroused your vagina will produce its own lubrication to prevent any friction, but there's also no shame in using some extra lube from a bottle. It's always useful to have lube, lube is great! Just make sure that it is water- or silicone-based and not oil-based. I wish I'd known this when my boyfriend and I used Vaseline (which is oil-based) as lube, the condom broke and I had to get the morning after pill. Fun times.

My tips for having non-painful sex:

lube   go slow

lots of foreplay

relax, breathe, and have fun

remember you can stop at any point

be in a position where
you are in control i.e. on top

Sex can hurt whether it's your first time or your 100ᵗʰ time, but if you are finding it painful a lot of the time then talk to your doctor about it. There are many reasons why it might be painful: some are serious, some aren't, and most are treatable. It's always good practice to get yourself checked out. Your sexual and genital health is just as important as your general health.

Will I bleed?

Back in the day (and still presently in some places around the world), a woman was expected to be a virgin when she got married. If she bled when she had sex on her wedding night then that was proof of her virginity. This sounds ridiculous to us now, it's important to know that there is no way to 'prove' virginity – no amount of bleeding or measuring someone's vagina can help you here. People think that they will bleed the first time they have penetrative sex because of the hymen. I remember for years thinking that the hymen was a full sheet-like membrane that 'broke'.

But that's not biologically the case, and I've no idea why we don't teach this to people. Last year, a friend of mine in her 20s lost her virginity with her boyfriend and before it happened, she came to me all worried asking about her hymen and if it would hurt when it broke. Here's the thing about the hymen – it only partially covers the vaginal opening and it's stretchy. Your hymen can be stretched by a penis, but also by tampons, fingers and even doing some sports. That sounds a lot less scary now, right? I remember being mind-blown when I learnt this, years after I'd actually had sex. But again, if you do find yourself regularly bleeding during sex then get yourself checked out by a doctor.

Will I fall in love?

This is one of my least favourite stereotypes about sex, especially because it is annoyingly grounded in some scientific fact. We wouldn't sometimes call it 'making love' if sex had no connection to love at all. You're not going to automatically fall in love with someone after having sex with them, it's not some magic spell, but it is likely to make you feel closer and more connected to them. Lots of hormones are released when you have sex and have an orgasm, and one of them, oxytocin, is what is responsible for this feeling, hence why it's referred to as the 'cuddle hormone'. The release of oxytocin triggers feelings of attachment and bonding which is why you feel all loved-up and cuddly after sex. And don't worry, you're not crazy – it's just your brain chemicals doing their thing.

Do I have to be in love?

Even though sex can create all those lovey-dovey feelings, you don't have to be in love to have sex. Some people prefer to wait until they're in a loving, stable relationship before having sex for the first time but not everyone does and that's fine. I personally think that you are more likely to have a positive experience the first time if you are in a caring relationship but that doesn't mean to say that people who do are better than people who don't. Everyone is on their own personal sexual journey, you may or may not be in love the first time you have sex – what's more important is trust, respect and communication, with any sexual partner.

What if I cum early?

Don't worry, this is completely normal and happens more often than people admit. It's difficult not to get embarrassed if this does happen but you should know that it's nothing to be ashamed of. Sex isn't an endurance test like you see in some porn. Also, it is quite likely that if you have a penis, the first time you have sex you will ejaculate quickly and that's fine. If you are with someone and they cum (or come) early, don't make them feel more embarrassed than they probably already feel. Don't laugh at them and make sure you tell them it's OK, because it is. If it becomes a recurring problem there are things you can do to prevent it, but the best thing is to talk to your partner.

What if I don't cum at all?

Also completely normal! Despite what porn would have us believe, only about 30 per cent of women orgasm through penetrative sex alone (more on this later ...).

What if I can't get it up?

Again, totally normal. Having sex for the first time can be a nervous and exciting experience and that can affect the functionality of your penis. Try to relax and take your time, there's no rush, you can take as long as you need. But don't blame it on condoms, they're important for protection against pregnancy and STIs. There are other ways to help with erection problems that don't involve putting yourself at risk by having unprotected sex.

What if it's bad and they dump me?

Well to be honest, then they're a horrible person. But try not to worry about being 'bad' at sex. It's your first time, no one expects you to be an expert lover. I generally take the stance that there's no such thing as someone being 'good' or 'bad' in bed, it's about the relationship and connection between two people. Whether they're a good fit, to put it crudely. And if the sex is bad the first time, don't worry, it will get better. Remember, it takes two to tango. If someone does dump you after having sex with you then that's awful, but it says a lot more about them than it does about you.

I'm [age], is it weird I haven't had sex yet?

No. No. No. It may feel like all your friends and everyone you know has already had sex but that's just not the case. Some people lie, and the people who haven't had sex either are probably keeping quiet just like you. It doesn't matter what age you are when you have sex for the first time, whether it's when you've reached the age of consent in your country or when you're a lot older. It doesn't make you any less of a person just because you haven't had sex. Be patient and kind to yourself, it may seem like the most important thing in the world but it's really not. (Why are you writing a whole book about it then Hannah?! Damn it.) Between 2010 and 2012, the British National Survey of Sexual Attitudes and Lifestyles (or Natsal) interviewed more than 15,000 men and women aged between 16 and 74. They discovered that only about 30 per cent of people aged between 16 and 24 had had sex under the age of 16. So far more people are talking about it than are actually doing it!

At school I remember obsessing over virginity. When I was going to lose it and to whom, which of my friends had already done the deed and which hadn't, who had done it with more than one person already. But all of that is just background noise. Ultimately it's your choice (and your partner's) when and how you have sex for the first time. Virginity is not a prize, or a symbol of shame. It can mean whatever you want it to mean, whether that's something really important to you or nothing at all. Your body is your body, you decide what you do with it. You should never be made to feel ashamed about when and how you lose your virginity. No matter what your gender or sexuality is, you know what is best for you.

Communicate that to your partner, and listen to them too.

Chapter 3

Four generations of Witton family sex ed

'I assume I learnt about sex from Mary Doyle'

I don't just want to reminisce over my own sex education and look forwards to how I would like sex education to be in the future. I also want to look back over previous generations, and find out what their experiences were like. So I sat down with my mum (53), then my gran (74), and then my great-grandma (102), to talk to them about how they learned about sex.

key

Mum = my mum

Nudy = my gran

Grandma = my great-grandma

Standad = my granddad, Nudy's husband

Boo = my great-granddad, Grandma's late husband

Nudy learned about sex from an older girl who lived opposite, 'I do remember being in Grandma and Boo's bed one morning and they were obviously preparing themselves to tell me about sex and I do remember saying, "oh it's alright, Mary's told me!"'

When I asked Grandma how she learned about sex, she said that she never spoke about it with her parents and that she learned everything from Boo. I asked her how Boo found out and she said, 'his family had a maid and when he was 16 she took him down the cellar and taught him.' Oh. My. God. I can't believe I heard these words coming from my Grandma's mouth. Amazing. The interview with my Grandma was a bit slow and stagnated because, well, she's old, and she couldn't remember much. But my absolute favourite thing she said was when she was talking about Boo. She said they fell in love straight away, 'he was playing piano and I fell in love. He was going with this other girl but he left her and went with me instead. And I left the other guy.' Juicy stuff. She talked about how experienced he was and mentioned that he always had a drawer full of condoms next to his bed. Grandma was quiet for a while (she needs a long time to think) and then she turned to me with this smile on her face and she didn't look 102 any more, she looked 25, and she said simply, 'I enjoyed it.'

Speaking of Grandma and Boo's condom collection, Nudy remembered that when she was about 14 she really wanted a younger brother. So she and her sister Ann found the stash of condoms, got a needle and pricked holes in them. But clearly it didn't work, because they didn't get a younger brother.

There was no sex education at school and so Nudy had to learn everything from either her friends or her parents. And sometimes relatives aren't always best-equipped to deal with this kind of thing. When Nudy started her period she was visiting her Auntie Marian in London, who was so embarrassed that she couldn't tell her husband what was happening and so made things up, such as Nudy having a tummy ache, to explain what was going on. One thing that I had no idea about was what pads used to be like – 'the sanitary towels had buttons, they were big. They went in your knickers but it buttoned to your sanitary belt and the loops buttoned on to that to hold it up.' What the hell is a sanitary belt? Buttons? Loops? It all sounds way too complicated. I am very grateful for the sanitary pad technology we have now. Nudy and my mum knew about periods before they got theirs but Grandma was less fortunate. She had no idea what was happening to her so she asked her brother! 'I went to my brother ... and I was bleeding and I asked him "Why am I bleeding?" Apparently he didn't have a clue either.

Mum said that she did get sex education at school but it came so late that she was already on the Pill and having sex when they had that lesson. Although before that, sex was something that was confusing to her. On a weekend away with her youth group she saw two people having sex, 'I just remember the sleeping bag going up and down ... and I couldn't work that out.'

My mum did then learn what it was all about, and her main piece of advice for myself and my sister when it came to sex was, 'if you're not comfortable farting in front of them, you're not ready to have sex.' Thanks Mum. Although when I think about it, that isn't bad advice. I asked all three of them if there was ever any mention of LGBTQ+ people in their sex education and my Grandma sums it up really, 'no! I didn't know anything about that. Good heavens no!' Even my mum, who grew up in the 1960s and '70s, had no idea about it until she went to a punk gig when she was 15 and saw two girls kissing. 'My mouth dropped open ... I hadn't even thought ... I hadn't heard anything against it, you know? I just didn't really know it existed.' Although she said that in school people would throw around the insult 'you're gay', she knew it was derogatory but didn't really understand what it meant. Even my sex education was LGBTQ+ -absent. I knew that gay people existed and that it was perfectly fine and normal, but there was never any specific education that would have helped the young LGBTQ+ people who were sitting in the classroom, and no education about what being transgender meant. There was a girl in my school who was trans but at the time none of us had the vocabulary or knowledge to understand it other than 'she was a boy and now she's a girl'. And even now the inclusion of LGBTQ+-specific information is missing from many young people's sex and relationship education.

My favourite thing that I learned during these interviews was how Nudy found out she was pregnant with my mother. Nudy and Standad got married in October 1962, right after the Cuban Missile Crisis – probably because they thought they were going to die at any minute. Oh, and also because they loved each other. I'd always wondered about this and Nudy confirmed it for me when she said that they were having sex before they got married. Rebels. The contraceptive Pill had become available in 1961 and so I asked if she used it, but apparently they would only give it to women who had already had children. When they went to the family planning clinic they had to prove that they were definitely going to get married and Nudy got a diaphragm, 'vile thing', she said. Unfortunately, Nudy got her period at her wedding – that sounds like a nightmare situation, especially in a white dress. A month later, her next period didn't come and she was worried because they didn't have much money and she was only 19. NINETEEN. (By my age, Nudy was married and had two kids.)

So she went back to the family planning clinic and this is the bit that shocked me: there weren't any ordinary tests like you can do now to see if you're pregnant. Because they had to inject a frog with something.

So I did a little research and here's what I found out …

> *In the early 20th century, medical research identified a hormone, human chorionic gonadotropin, or hCG, that's only found in pregnant women. To test for the presence of hCG, a sample of the woman's urine was injected into an immature female mouse, frog or rabbit and if hCG was present in the urine sample, the animal would go into heat. The test is known as the Aschheim-Zondek test and is about 98 per cent accurate.*
>
> *As mentioned by Marc Lallanilla in his article "A Brief History of Pregnancy Tests"*

And now we just pee on a stick. Modern medicine eh?

Because the clinic Nudy went to didn't have any frogs, they had to use other, less reliable, methods. The nurse examined her and told her she was pregnant because she had 'active nipples'. And so my grandparents stopped using contraception because they thought they were pregnant and then, you guessed it, she got pregnant.

If you and your family members are comfortable doing so, I would highly recommend talking to them about their sex education. Especially your grandparents, because the stories are just so good! It really put a lot into perspective about how far we've come, medically and socially.

Chapter 4

LGBTQ+

I'm a straight cis woman. I'm attracted to the opposite sex, and the sex I was assigned at birth matches my gender identity, so there are a lot of things that I don't have to think about when it comes to sexuality, dating, socialising, my body, friends and family. Because of this privilege, and my lack of personal experience on all things LGBTQ+, I've invited some of my friends to write about it and tell their stories themselves. But first, let's start by looking at what LGBTQ+ actually means.

L Lesbian

G Gay

B Bisexual

T Transgender

Q Queer / questioning

+ so many other things !

There are many differing opinions within the LGBT community about whether the Q and the + should be included, and also about the addition of other letters (A for Asexual, I for Intersex and even another A for Ally). Some people have started using 'GSM' – Gender Sexuality Minority – instead, but it seems that in the mainstream, at least for now, 'LGBT' is most commonly understood.

At school, I remember being taught that gay people existed and that it was fine, but I don't remember there being any kids in my year who 'came out'. That was 10 years ago though, so I hope more young people now feel comfortable and safe enough in their school environment to be themselves. But there is a definite lack of sex education in general at school, and more specifically a lack of any kind of sex education that isn't about heterosexual relationships.

Acknowledging the existence of gay people isn't enough, there's so much more to cover. Information like the fact that there's a difference between your sex, gender, sexual orientation, romantic orientation and sexual behaviour, is rarely taught in schools.

Biological Sex

(Bio-sex)

This refers to your biological sex, which can usually be determined by three things – your genitals (penis/vagina), hormones (testosterone/oestrogen) and chromosomes (XY/XX). At birth a baby is assigned a sex that is either 'male' or 'female'. But there are not just two sexes. Some people (about 1 in 2,000 births) are intersex which is a general term used to describe someone whose genitals, reproductive system, hormones and · chromosomes aren't necessarily wholly 'male' or 'female'. For example, someone could have a penis but XX (female) chromosomes, a vagina and XY (male) chromosomes, or ambiguous genitals. There are many different variations but not all are visible. Some intersex people don't know that they are intersex until puberty, and some people may never know.

Even though it's not very common, it is still important to understand that even within biology, sex is not as simple as just 'male' and 'female'.

Gender

Gender is different to sex. Your gender is about how you identify, and how you feel. There are different ways in which you can identify with your gender.

Cis gender = your gender identity matches the sex you were assigned at birth.

Transgender = your gender identity does not match the sex you were assigned at birth. For example, if you were born a boy but identify as female. Often transgender people will transition but everyone's transition is different. It could be changing your name, using different pronouns, dressing differently, taking hormones, or surgery.

Non-binary = this means not identifying as male or female. 'Male' and 'female' are at opposite ends of the gender binary spectrum but there's a whole host of sexes, genders and identities in between, for example gender queer, gender fluid, etc.

Gender expression is also different to gender identity. There are many symbols and signifiers in society that communicate your gender to other people. This could be the clothes you wear or how you do your hair or makeup. Gender identity is internal, gender expression is external and the two don't necessarily have to match up. You can be a boy who wears makeup, a girl with short hair, you can have a more androgynous style or move between masculine and feminine depending on the day.

The outward expression of gender is the easiest way to determine a person's gender when you first meet them. If you are unsure, then ask how a person identifies and which pronouns they use. If you get it wrong, don't make a big deal out of it. Simply apologise and correct yourself.

Gender is a spectrum and it's not as simple as vagina = woman or penis = man. How someone identifies may be different to the body that they have, and how they choose to transition, if at all, is completely up to them.

Juno Dawson on *Being Transgender*

While acknowledging gender is 100 per cent made-up bollocks, I was undeniably more drawn to clothes, hair and makeup assigned to the female sex. This started with toys when I was little, and all of my role models were female characters. It was with a real resignation that I lived as a boy. When I was little, understanding of transgender issues was non-existent. There was little representation in the media, and what there was was wholly negative. I figured that most gay people just wanted to be the opposite sex.

Later, as I met transgender people, I realised that there are infinite options beyond the binary. For me, it's an open-and-shut case: I really feel there was an administrative error and, had all been fair in the universe, I would have been born with female chromosomes and organs. Technically I am a transsexual – I'm not just changing my gender, I'm also changing sex through hormone therapy.

However before I started to change sex, I had already changed gender. My hair, clothes, passport, name and bank accounts were all female before I even swallowed an oestrogen pill. We are all free to experiment and play with traditional notions of male and female. If we rigidly adhere to what boys and girls are 'supposed' to do, gender stereotypes will never change – and no one benefits from outmoded gender expectations.

Being trans isn't easy. Although we've come a long way as a community, many people are grotesquely small-minded. Transphobia is a daily occurrence – not necessarily in terms of violence or verbal abuse, but in terms of simply living in a world that hasn't really made room for us yet. Making life easier for trans people starts with everyone rebelling against gender binaries.

Juno Dawson (@junodawson) writes full time and lives in Brighton. She loves *Doctor Who*, is a keen follower of horror films and connoisseur of pop music, and is a School Role Model for Stonewall. In 2015, Juno announced her intention to undergo gender transition and live as a woman.

Riley Dennis on Dating While Trans

For cisgender people, announcing what genitals you have the moment you meet someone would be considered pretty weird. Can you imagine? 'Hi, I'm Riley, and I have a penis.'

But for trans people, that's basically what we have to do in the dating world. The little 'I'm trans' note on our dating profiles is there to tell cis people we might not have the genitals they were expecting. I, and probably a lot of other trans people, would prefer not to have to do that – but it's a defence mechanism. Trans people are regularly attacked, verbally and physically, for what cis people say is us 'tricking them'. So many of us try to be clear from the beginning: Yes, I'm trans. If my genitals bother you, move along. For this reason, and many others, dating as a trans person can be a bizarre and confusing process. In most cases, when strangers ask me about my genitals (it's a pretty regular occurrence as a trans person), I don't want to talk about it. It's not anyone's business but my own and the people I might be having sex with. However, I do think it's reasonable (although also extremely awkward, and not totally socially acceptable yet) to discuss genitals with people I might end up sleeping with. I get it, you want to know what you're working with.

Trans people also have to be constantly aware of whether they're 'passing' or not – that is, if the majority of folks around them are perceiving them as cis. I hate the concept of passing, but it's one we can't seem to avoid. Cis people are obsessed with whether or not we 'look cis'. To be clear:

trans people don't have a 'look', and neither do cis people. Some trans people 'look' cis, some 'look' trans – and for some people, it depends on who's looking. As a non-binary trans woman who people often think looks trans, or looks like a man, my role in this is different than some other trans folks. For trans women who 'pass' as cis women, they often have to out themselves as trans. For trans women who don't 'pass', we often have to prove that we're 'woman enough'. We have to wear makeup all the time and overly perform our femininity because we 'look masculine'. As soon as I'm makeup-less and in sweats, people question if I'm really trans or not. Trans men face many of the same difficulties, but in the other direction. And non-binary folks are often expected to constantly look androgynous.

In the dating world, being trans complicates things because we often define our sexual orientation by the gender or genders we're attracted to – and by their genitals. But sex doesn't always look like we think it does. Sometimes gay sex is penis in vagina. Sometimes straight sex is two people with vaginas. That's jarring for a lot of people who've defined their sexual identities around the genitals they're attracted to. I don't want to make it sound like dating as a trans person is impossible. Lots of us find great, amazing partners, and there are so many happy trans people out there. But I'm still looking forward to the day when we care a little less about genitals and a little more about finding someone we actually like.

Riley J. Dennis (@RileyJayDennis) is a YouTuber, activist and public speaker. She identifies as a non-binary lesbian and strives to make her version of feminism as intersectional as possible.

Roly on Being Gender Fluid

Identifying as Gender Fluid has been one of the most confusing yet liberating things I've dealt with.

I'm so happy with who I am now but this has not always been the case. From the very beginning, trying to differentiate between my gender expression and identity was something I've found hard. Coupled with simultaneously trying to accept my sexuality, it's safe to say I was a rather messed-up child. As someone who looks like a man regardless of what I do, I've been told many times that I'm just a very feminine gay boy and this has nothing to do with gender. Growing up, I also lived in an area where being gay is one thing, but crossing the line into gender bending will get you abused openly in the streets.

I really wish schools had been more open to discussing gender and gender fluidity back when I was young. We only got taught about cis, heterosexual relationships – nothing else. At school, I also had a really hard time with bullying. Most days I would be beaten up and have abuse thrown my way. All this together made me push all these feelings away, and do anything just to fit in. It took me a long time to come out as gay, but even after accepting this there was still something inside me I could not work out. However, when I moved to London with my YouTube friends, I started to experiment with dressing in girls' clothes and using makeup. It was a weird feeling being with people completely free from judgement and it was the most eye-opening experience. I was so used to being told what I could and could not wear and do I had almost forgotten what real happiness felt like. I was trying to work out what I did identify as, because my feelings seemed to change from day to day, so I searched different genders online and came across 'gender fluid'. BAM! It was like fireworks going off in my head, like YES! This is me, this is how I feel. Fast-forward to now, I know moving away was the best thing I did. I'd no idea how unhappy I was back in Devon and how much it was holding me back. Being free to be whoever I want to be is the best feeling, and not letting my gender determine anything I do has opened up a completely new world to me.

I want people to know that you don't need to look a certain way to identify as being a non-binary gender. Don't let anyone define your identity, no matter what. I am so proud to represent the + in the LGBTQ+ community, and I will always be a voice for the people who can't understand their genders.

Being gender fluid is one of the most confusing things I have ever had to deal with, but I would not change it for the world.

Roly (@RolyUnGashaa) is a genderfluid YouTuber and activist living in London. He has a passion for everything LGBTQ+ and uses his channel to help others accept their identities.

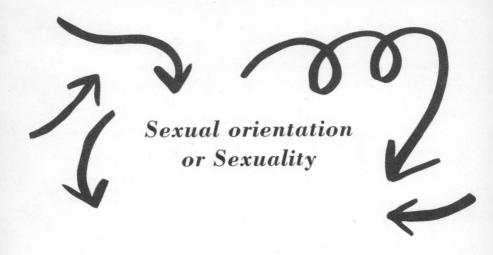

Sexual orientation or Sexuality

This refers to who you're sexually attracted to, who you get turned on by and who you can imagine yourself being with sexually. Here are the basics.

heterosexual
= attracted to people of the opposite gender to your own.

homosexual
= attracted to people of the same gender as yourself.

bisexual
= attracted to two genders.

pansexual
= attracted to all genders.

Whatever your orientation, it is completely normal. Who you are attracted to is not something you choose, it's part of who you are. Love is love. Just as with gender, sexuality is a spectrum. The simplest way to demonstrate this is by using the Kinsey Scale. Alfred Kinsey was a pioneering scientist who extensively studied human sexuality in the mid-20th century. The Kinsey Scale goes from 1 to 6: 1 is 100 per cent heterosexual, 6 is 100 per cent homosexual, and 2–5 are different variations and intensities of sexual fluidity or bisexuality. I think that I'm probably a 2 on the Kinsey Scale and sometimes I like to say that I'm 'hetero-flexible'.

Sexuality is not just about who you're attracted to but about the extent of your sexual desire in the first place. Having sexual feelings for other people is seen as the norm, but what about the people who don't experience sexual attraction?

The definition of 'asexuality' is the lack of sexual attraction to anyone. Sexual orientation and romantic orientation are different; often they match up, but not necessarily. Asexual people can still experience romantic attraction. There are also aromantic people who don't experience romantic attraction. And just as with everything else, asexuality is also on a spectrum.

Rowan Ellis on *The Difficulties of Dating as a Queer Woman*

There's a saying in the LGBTQ+ community: 'Dating while queer is like finding a job; you either have to do it online or get referred'. As a queer woman I know that this is a strange reality to find yourself in. If you're straight you can be out walking your dog, or in a Starbucks, or on a spaceship, and there will be people that you can just assume are straight too. The only issue is whether they are single and into you specifically. And although you might face the bitter sting of rejection if you ask, it's unlikely to be a dangerous situation for you. Attempting to date while queer is slightly different.

Let's start with the numbers. Statistically, there are fewer of us; it's harder to even find someone to ask on a date, let alone to find someone you like who likes you back. In a lot of cases there are enough queer people to be present, but not quite enough to be visible. Unlike many other marginalised groups, a large number of LGBTQ+ people have the superpower of invisibility. We can decide who knows what lies behind the Clark Kent glasses and when they find out. Often this is a necessity to keep us safe. However, it also lays the burden of coming out on each of us. So maybe you decide to go down the route of sticking to LGBTQ+ only spaces, because at least there you know everyone is safe. The problem is ... what LGBTQ+ spaces can you find? Well, almost exclusively you're looking at 18+ places with alcohol, like bars and clubs, in big towns and cities. Good luck finding a date for prom, kids. Supposedly, the rise of dating apps has been a game changer for queer women, allowing you to connect with other women near you. However, apps for queer women tend to be peppered with (heterosexual) guys looking for threesomes with their girlfriends. Boo! The sexual commodification and objectification of queer women (for example, the fact that lesbian porn is produced seemingly solely for straight men), spills out into these spaces that were meant to be ours. Ultimately, also, when you make profiles on queer dating apps and websites, you are outing yourself online. Although it seems like a safe bubble, where you can feel giddy talking to a cute girl, these profiles can be seen by anyone. It's awful to contemplate, but that in and of itself can potentially be dangerous – for example, after the homophobic gay propaganda law was enacted in Russia, we saw online profiles being used to lure gay men into violence and abuse. More recently, at the 2016 Olympics in Rio, a 'journalist' lured queer male athletes into meeting him via Grindr, and proceeded to out them online. The journalist seemed surprised, and even judgemental, that gay men were using this app, and he seemingly had no awareness of its necessity.

In the end, our source of love, friendship and community often comes from pockets of mutual friends finding mutual friends. Private Facebook groups for people who share identities flourish, as young LGBTQ+ people find spaces to socialise without the pressures of a sexualised, alcohol-driven environment. All of us, regardless of our gender or sexuality, need to understand the importance of queer community spaces, apps and websites, and support them however we can.

Rowan Ellis (@HeyRowanEllis) runs a YouTube channel where she critiques media and popular culture through a feminist and queer lens. She helped to found the FemTube movement supporting women creators on YouTube, and runs the fortnightly #femtubechat.

Alayna Fender on *Being Bisexual*

The path to figuring out my sexuality was not a straight one (ha). As a woman who finds herself attracted to men, women, and everyone in between, the identifier I use is bisexual. However, there are a couple of other labels that I could fall under. By definition, I am pansexual. I am also a part of the queer community. The identifier I use most often is 'bi', because I find it the simplest, and the easiest for others to understand. However, the bi in bi-sexuality indicates two. An attraction to two genders, most often assumed to be male and female. Because of this, the pansexual label, which acknowledges attraction to genders other than simply 'male' and 'female', is much more fitting for me.

Why then do I choose to identify as bi? Because my personal definition of bisexuality includes being attracted to my own gender, as well as other genders. Using this definition, the label of bisexual suits me well.

It took me years to figure out that I wasn't straight. I had crushes on boys throughout my school years, but without realising it, I was also doing the same thing with women. I used to have this picture of Kristen Stewart up on my bedroom wall. I didn't know who she was, I had just seen her picture in a magazine, cut it out and put it up. When my friends came over I would show them the picture and say, 'Isn't she beautiful? She's the most beautiful woman I've ever seen!' Thinking that every girl felt the same way that I did. And they'd respond, 'Yeah she's pretty.' And I'd say, 'No, she's gorgeous.' Not quite understanding that I had the hots for Kristen Stewart, and my girlfriends didn't. In middle school, I had boyfriends. I had my first kiss with a boy. It was all very exciting. I told my friends and we giggled and discussed every detail. Nothing was out of place. Nothing seemed odd.

It was high school when I had my first romantic experience with a girl. I told my best friend about it at the time, and she got incredibly angry with me. I remember her being disgusted, and making me promise to never do anything like that again. It was awful, and my first experience of the dichotomy that exists in the lives of bisexual people. I kiss a boy, and everyone is excited. I kiss a girl, and I'm disgusting, clearly only doing it to attract the attention of more boys. Looking back on it now it all makes a lot of sense, but back then I didn't understand. I thought my feelings for girls 'didn't count' because only feelings for boys were legitimate. I thought my actions with girls were sinful and wrong, because only heterosexual experiences were allowed. I thought all girls had the same feelings for other girls as I did, but just didn't act on them.

It was thanks to YouTube and the plethora of information and community there that I learned the term 'bisexual'. And that's when I figured it out. It finally clicked that I didn't have to be gay or straight, I could be somewhere in the middle.

Alayna Fender (@MissFenderr) is a cat-loving LGBTQ+ YouTube content creator from Canada. She's been making videos in various bedrooms, wearing various cat shirts, for her MissFenderr and MissAlaynaa channels since 2012.

Amelia Morris *on Asexuality*

If somebody is asexual, it means they don't experience sexual attraction. Simple enough! However, it can be very difficult to work out exactly what sexual attraction is, particularly if you don't experience it. In basic terms, sexual attraction is when you feel a pull or desire to be sexually intimate with somebody. For lots of people, this attraction is triggered by the other person's physical appearance. It can be also be triggered by somebody's actions, voice, or other characteristics.

Every asexual person's experience of sex is different, of course, but one thing that unifies them is that the experience of sexual attraction I've just described doesn't happen to them.

Notice that I didn't say that asexual people don't want to have sex, or don't have romantic relationships. Lots of people like to define asexuality that way, but it's just not true. Being asexual isn't the same thing as being abstinent or celibate. Abstinence and celibacy are about a lack of sexual activity, not sexual attraction. Asexual people might choose to have sex for a variety of reasons.

To begin with, they might just enjoy having sex. Sex can be really fun, you don't need to be sexually attracted to your partner (or partners) for that to be the case. Some asexual people find that the emotional intimacy of sex makes it enjoyable for them. They don't need sexual attraction for that, either. Sometimes, an asexual person might have sex because their non-asexual partner wants to have sex.

So long as the non-asexual person isn't guilting or coercing their partner into it, this is a perfectly valid choice, too. If you're struggling to work out if you're asexual, it's a good idea to keep the following things in mind: sexual, romantic and aesthetic attraction don't always coexist. Most people agree that you can want to have sex with somebody without wanting to start a relationship with them. This also works the other way around – you can feel romantic attraction (a desire to be romantic or start a relationship with someone) without wanting to have sex with them.

Have you ever been drawn to a painting or sculpture just because it's beautiful? That's aesthetic attraction. You can feel like that about people, too. It's easy to get muddled and think that you can't be asexual because you're able to appreciate when people are good-looking. But you can think somebody's cute without wanting to have sex with them. Asexuality is pretty rare, as sexual orientations go. But the community is becoming more visible day by day, and asexuality is being taken more seriously as a result. If you're struggling with your asexuality, remember that you're not 'broken' or 'wired wrong.'

You're ace!

Amelia Morris (@AmeliaAce_) is an active member of the asexual community and vlogs about asexuality on her channel AmeliaAce.

Labels are a **FUNNY** ONE. *Just because you fit a certain* **LABEL** **doesn't** *necessarily* **mean** *you have* **to** *identify with it.*

Ash Hardell on *Identity*

A mysterious subject I find myself constantly investigating, both in life and on my YouTube channel, is the concept of identity. It is mind-blowingly complex, there are an infinite amount of qualifiers a person can choose to identify with. Some of my labels of choice include: queer, bi, pan, a woman, sister, daughter, wife, student of life, an activist, optimist, traveller, hopeless romantic, and YouTuber. Another aspect of identity I'm fascinated with is that it isn't fixed. As we learn, grow, and change, so does the way we identify, and that's what I want to talk about here; how to navigate and explore a fluid identity as we adventure through life. So if you've ever found yourself struggling with the age-old question; 'WHO AM I?!' sit back and relax, because I have some tips for you.

First, understand that only you have power over your identity. As we go through life we are going to encounter an endless number of different labels, and that can be both scary and exciting. Some identifiers will be like gifts. For example in high school I was labelled 'a creative.' Which was fantastic because, as I constantly ping-ponged from theatre to speech to film to drawing, I never knew what to call myself. An actor? Maybe some days. A photographer? Others. But once my artistically fluid self was deemed 'a creative,' I was finally at peace. Not all labels will be gifts however. Others will be thrust upon us. For me, 'bisexual' was a word people used to label me with when I first came out as being attracted to more than one gender. That word never felt right to me, though, and a few years later, I stumbled across the term pansexual, which was much more fitting. However, being labelled bisexual was what initially helped me explore and enter the LGBTQ+ community, so I will always have a connection to the word. In the end, you get to pick which words stick, and even what those words mean. My bi or pan might be different to yours, and that's OK. You're also allowed to alter your definitions as you gain life experience. It's your identity and you have the power.

My next tip, which I'm borrowing from the fantastic Dr Lindsey Doe, is stay curious. One of my favourite ways to learn about my identity is to learn about other peoples' identities. In high school I did this by simply showing up and interacting with everyone who also happened to be there: jocks, dancers, academics, etc. In college exploring my identity was easy because I was surrounded by others who were doing the same thing. I was also immersed in social justice and women's studies classes that introduced me to a variety of new ways of viewing the world. Once I left, however, things got a little tricky. Post undergrad, I began settling into a routine. I went to work, I came home and I was surrounded by the same people every day, who were older and settled and stable in their identities. Unlike them, however, I didn't feel like I was done changing. I had to learn how to keep growing even though I had a degree, a job, an apartment, and was considered by many already 'grown up'. I did this in a variety of ways; I took to the Internet, devoured TED talks, became an active creator and consumer in feminist blogging circles, volunteered at queer organisations that I thought could teach me about diversity, attended workshops and talks about gender and race, joined book clubs and visited therapy to learn about ways to stay mentally healthy. I ultimately found out that a massive amount of knowledge was out there for me if I had the bravery and the time to look for it. Just because college was over didn't mean my education was.

Next, explore. Different parts of your identity will come out in different situations, SO TRY LOTS OF THINGS! This could mean immersing yourself in clubs, activities, sports, daily routines, wearing different clothes or even testing out certain mindsets. If you think you might potentially be interested in a lifestyle or outlook, dive into it, if only for a week, to test it out. I tried being vegetarian, it lasted three years, and although it wasn't ultimately for me, it did teach me how important it is to be a socially conscious and responsible consumer. That is a lesson I take to the grocery store with me every week. One afternoon shopping, I wandered into the men's section of a department store, I found a comfy shirt I liked, then a style I liked, and later a word to describe that style: androgynous. Then I learned there are many other words for people who don't fit into gender norms. Quickly I became an ally and activist for anyone who felt this way, and my YouTube channel morphed into a space which campaigned for equal rights and visibility for minorities and grew to have more than 250,000 community members ... all because one day I tried something new and put on a shirt from the guys' section.

I'm no expert on identity, but the best piece of advice I can offer you is don't ever feel stuck. Stay curious, and explore any identity you desire. And don't worry if you ever feel overwhelmed with labels and qualifiers because remember, only you have power over your identity. You pick your labels, you choose their definitions, and I promise, it's a fun and exciting journey doing so.

Ash Hardell (@AshHardell) is a 24-year-old, queer YouTuber who likes to drink beer, kiss her wife, and talk about life on the Internet.

Coming out

*I*n our society, being heterosexual and cis is what's seen as the norm. It's 'straight until proven otherwise.' The assumption that everyone is straight, the assumption that when we see a man and a woman together we think 'couple' and when we see two people of the same gender together we think 'friends,' and the lack of visibility and representation of LGBTQ+ people in the media, feeds into what we call 'heteronormativity.'

And because of this, to have any kind of visibility, LGBTQ+ people need to 'come out.' Some people argue that the whole concept of coming out is a heteronormative idea in itself, some people never announce their sexuality or gender and just get on with their lives, some shout it from the rooftops, others have quiet conversations with some friends and family but not others, some people make YouTube videos about it! The first thing you need to know is that whether you come out or not, and however you wish to do that, is entirely up to you. You should never feel like you *have* to disclose your sexuality to anyone – you can be out and proud or you can still be proud but just not out to the world.

Coming out isn't just a singular event, either, it's a process and you can take as much time as you need. Usually the first time you come out will be to yourself. Maybe you've known all along or maybe you've suppressed it for a long time, but the first person you need to tell and to ask for love and acceptance from is you. And for some people this can be much easier said than done. Just remember that whatever your gender or sexuality, you are wonderful and deserve love as much as the next person.

There's no right or wrong way to come out. I know people who have blurted it out, texted it, written it down on a piece of paper and left the room as someone read it, or who came out by introducing their girlfriend/boyfriend – however you feel comfortable expressing yourself is the right way for you. But if you're worried about someone's reaction then here's the best advice I can give you:

Build a support network before you come out to the person/people you're most worried about. This can be made of friends, family members, or people online who know and will be there for you practically and emotionally. You need a safety net, especially if the people you're worried about coming out to are the people who you live with and who pay for your home and food. You can find support online, in local LGBTQ+ youth groups, through charities, friends in school, or maybe you've got a gay relative. The support network is for the worst-case scenario and hopefully it won't come to that. Your family and friends should love you no matter what; for some of them it might be a lot to process, but give them time. They could just be confused or scared, and even though it might be you that needs support right now, try to answer their questions and help them understand. It's not your responsibility to do that, so don't feel obliged if you don't want to, but it will help the relationship.

Throughout your life you may find yourself coming out over and over again. When you tell new friends or colleagues about your partner, when a stranger assumes you're straight, when someone uses the wrong pronouns. It can be annoying and exhausting but unfortunately this is the world we live in. Hopefully you can find pride and happiness in being out. Being yourself, and unafraid and proud of expressing who you really are, can be one of the most liberating feelings.

After all, love is love.

What does the LGBTQ+ community mean to you?

I make a lot of videos about sex and relationships on my YouTube channel – it's something that my audience and I feel passionate about – and a large number of my audience are LGBTQ+. I turned to my Twitter followers and asked 'what does the LGBTQ+ community mean to you?' I got more than 100 replies (thank you!) and here are some of my favourites:

@lukesnotshady
A safe place, no fear of being judged or harassed

anonymous
It means that I have a place where I belong, I have people who are like me and I don't feel left out

@guccibdawg
It's a place of comfort in totally being yourself and knowing you'll be accepted and supported

@magic_blue_box
Meeting other people like me (asexual) so I don't feel like I'm alone anymore

@anya_morley
Somewhere everyone is supported and can know that it's OK not to be straight (something I've struggled a lot with)

@OfficialMadMan_
A place where you can be proud of who you are

@hurricane_ang
A safe space where I'm always accepted
even when I struggle to accept myself
thanks to societal conditioning

@finaljade
A place for me to be
myself without feeling
like I have to explain
myself constantly

@NickehBee
A safe space where I can be myself and where people with
similar experiences understand me and show love

@lesbianswbu
It means everything,
a family

@Breezio
A group of friendly, likeminded
people that preach acceptance
& making the world a brighter,
more fabulous place

@Siobhanisboring
It means safety and support. It means being able
to look around and see people like me. It means
happiness and it means hope

@Malene_Simonsen
Acceptance and friends. It's where I've met
some of the most amazing people and have
been able to be who I am

@hayleyharp
For me, it's a
place where
differences are
celebrated and
I can be my
authentic self

@wildfordodie
It's a place where I can learn and
become a more educated person!

@simplyimiread
This community gives me
confidence in the validity of
who I am & pride in being part
of such a constructive force

@bigworldsa
The LGBTQ+ community has
always been a place I ran to
when I felt hella alone and
different from everybody

@trucesteph
A place to go for help, no matter what the issue is

@kogucik13
It gives me courage to truly be myself and lets me know that I finally belong somewhere where I am loved

@sophtwareslumpp
It means whenever I see a rainbow flag a weight's lifted off my shoulders, it makes me feel safer

@curious_lenny
To me, it means a place of acceptance, but also a place of learning and personal growth

@frankcastlc
It means not feeling lost and alone. It means knowing you aren't broken. It means knowing who you are and loving who you are

@helenalv15
To me, the community is family. We don't all have supportive families, so we are there for each other instead

@Charli_TAW
I learnt about my identity through the community & it helped me come out. While it has problems, it's important!

@HannahDoldrums
A group of people who support anyone, especially the people who didn't get support from the people around them

@dftba Darling
The LGBTQ+ community is a family and a constant reminder I'm not alone. It means I can find people who see me

@0 Shine_Bright 0
The group of people who told me that there wasn't something wrong with me for liking boys and girls

@NeveAtkinson22
The community has really helped me to become a far more open minded person due to its presence on social media

And I think @bigsizz1 sums it up, the community is Love <3

How to be a good ally

So I've mentioned it before, but I'm straight and cis. And there are certain privileges that come with that. Here are just a few:

I've always felt normal because I've always learned about and seen examples of heterosexuality everywhere – my parents, friends, news, books, TV, films, etc.

I've never been bullied because of my sexuality or gender.

I've never feared that my parents might kick me out because of my sexuality or gender.

I can use the women's bathroom freely and without fear.

I can go to any country in the world and my sexuality isn't a crime.

Sometimes it can be hard at first to realise that you have a straight or cis privilege because your sexuality or gender is something you've rarely thought about. But that's exactly it, you've never had to think about it, and that's a privilege.

So here are some ways that us hetero-cis folk can help our LGBTQ+ friends and be the best allies to them:

1

Check your privilege. We just did that but it's always good to reiterate. Recognising your own privilege can help you to step outside yourself, see how the situation may be different for LGBTQ+ people and empathise with them. *Empathy is super-important in being a good ally.*

2

Listen. This step is also known as 'shut your mouth'. One of the best ways to be an ally is simply to listen to the people you're trying to help. *Let them tell you about their experiences rather than assuming what it's like to be them.* And it's not enough to just listen; you have to believe them. If someone tells you that they were a victim of homophobic bullying, don't say, 'but are you sure it was homophobic?' That's not listening.

Amplify others' voices. OK, so even though a lot of your role as an ally is to be quiet and listen, there are times when you should shout from the rooftops. Some straight people are more likely to listen to me than someone who is LGBTQ+ and so I should use that privilege to raise LGBTQ+ voices and share their stories. *This does not mean speaking over them or for them.* I've tried to practise this here by having some of my LGBTQ+ friends write about their own experiences. And so hopefully their stories will be read by lots of people.

3

Educate yourself. This can be through books, documentaries, the news, blogs, YouTube videos, even Tumblr. You can't rely on the LGBTQ+ people you know to answer every question that you have. Yes, they may be happy to help and impart their wisdom but they may not want to keep explaining how and why they're oppressed, and it's not their responsibility to educate you. *So be a good ally and do your research.*

4

5 **_This is not your time to shine._** No matter how much of an attention seeker you are (like myself), you are in a supporting role. You are not the star here. You are not the leading actor or director. You are the runner on set taking orders, listening to others, and making sure everyone is happy and well-hydrated.

6 **_Don't take breaks._** Do you think oppression takes a break? No. _And the LGBTQ+ people who are affected by this oppression certainly can't take a break from it._ So if you want to be a good ally you can't retreat back into your safe cosy place of privilege, you need to always be there for people who need the support.

7 **_Learn how to say sorry._** This is an important skill to have when you're dealing with social issues, especially things that you don't necessarily have personal experience of. You might mess up at some point – say or do the wrong thing – and so you need to learn how to apologise properly. _This means owning up to your mistakes, listening when you've been called out on something, learning from it and promising not to do it again._ Simple.

LGBTQ+ is wonderful, beautiful, diverse and loving. You are normal. You are not alone. There has been so much progress in the last 100 years in terms of LGBTQ+ rights and representation but there's still a long way to go, especially globally. There's loads of support out there and there'll be links to some useful websites at the end of this book.

And I know I've said it a million times but I feel like it's important to remind everyone again: Love is Love.

Chapter 5

consent

When I was in school, all I was taught about consent was 'no means no'.

Whilst that's true, it is certainly not enough education to really understand consent.

What is it? How do you give consent? How do you make sure you have consent? Consent in a sexual context should be simple – if everyone is into it, no one is being forced or pressured and everyone has the full capacity to consent, then you're good to go. But the reality is a lot more complex than that because we live in a society where sex is still taboo and a lot of people feel uncomfortable talking about it. However, communication is at the heart of consent, so we need to learn how to talk about it.

Sex where there is a lack of consent is not sex. It's sexual abuse or rape. It's a myth that most cases of rape are acts of extreme violence by a stranger. The perpetrator is much more likely to be someone you know (a partner, ex-partner, friend, colleague, etc.) and it can involve coercion, manipulation and maybe alcohol or drugs. I want everyone to feel in control of their bodies and what they do with them, to have a sense of body autonomy and the confidence to express what they want and don't want. This is so important, whether you're in a long-term relationship or having casual sex. There need to be open lines of communication, and you should feel comfortable enough with that person to be able to say 'no' if you don't want to do something. I've heard many stories from friends and online about people who don't want to do something but they 'go along with it' because it's easier than saying 'no'. This makes me so sad.

Why do we find it so hard to talk about consent in the bedroom? I don't know about you but for me personally I would much rather have the conversation and maybe not have sex than have sex not really knowing if the other person is into it. You know what's hot? Having sex with someone who very enthusiastically shows how much they clearly want to have sex with you too. Oh. My. God.

So here's your Consent 101:

Consent is ...

A voluntary, enthusiastic yes
Un-assumed
Mandatory

Consent can be ...

Verbal
Non-verbal
Withdrawn at any point
For some things and not others

No means no

If you hear a no, that's a no. A 'no' isn't a challenge; it isn't a case of pestering them enough to turn the 'no' into a 'yes'. That's not cool. Don't do that. Listen to your partner and if they say 'no' then respect their choice and don't force them. That's rape.

Other things that also mean 'no':

I don't feel like it

Not tonight

I'm not sure

I'm not feeling well

I don't know

Silence

This last one is especially important. Silence, or a lack of a 'no', does not equal a 'yes'. People often speak of the 'fight or flight' response in dangerous situations but they forget to mention 'freeze', and this is a very common response to uncomfortable or scary situations including sexual abuse. So if your partner is quiet, frozen or unresponsive, check in with them, see if they're OK.

Yes means yes

So instead of going ahead unless you hear 'no', look out for a 'yes'. Consent is a voluntary, enthusiastic and clear 'yes, I want this'.

What does a 'yes' sound like?

Yes please

That feels good

I'd like that!

I want you to touch me here

Keep going

Right there

I really want to have sex with you

Consent is sexy! But it's also mandatory. Remember you can consent to some things and not others, you can consent to something one time but not another, and you can change your mind. Consent should never be assumed because you're in a relationship, because you've done it before or because of a person's sexual history. You should always get consent – every time and for everything.

Some people think that this makes sex robotic or like a business deal, and it takes away the passion if you have to be constantly checking in. But when I hear people being reluctant to make sure their partner is into it, that's a massive red flag for me. Being 100 per cent sure that your partner is down is not only necessary, it allows you to relax and fully enjoy the experience. Consent can also be non-verbal too, and communicated through body language. Is your partner playing an active role or is it something that's just happening to them? Pay attention to body language and read signals. If you're unsure at any point, stop and ask.

How to ask for consent

If in doubt, ask. If in doubt, ask! If in doubt, ask! I don't know how to reiterate this enough. Ask ask ask. Communication is fantastic!

Do you like that?

Where do you want me to touch you?

How does that feel?

Are you OK?

Do you want this?

Tell me what you want

Shall I keep going?

Are you enjoying yourself?

How far do you want to go?

Situations where consent cannot happen

To confuse you even more (but don't worry, it's pretty simple) there are situations where, even if someone says 'yes', they cannot consent.

1

If they are under the age of consent and you are above it

The age of consent varies between countries, so make sure you're clued in. *No matter how mature a person seems or how much they say they are ready and want to have sex, legally they cannot consent.* You may think that, because the age is different in other countries, the number is arbitrary but it's the law. *So stick to it.*

2

If they are drunk or high

Yes, a lot of sex occurs when people have been drinking or taking drugs but when a person is incapacitated, they cannot consent. If someone can't walk straight, is slurring their words, can't stand up, or is slipping in and out of consciousness. *They are in a vulnerable state and need looking after.*

3

If there is a power imbalance

This is if someone is in a position of authority, such as a teacher, doctor, therapist, etc, over the other person. *It could even be a celebrity you admire.* The reason someone can't consent in these situations is because with power dynamics come vulnerabilities, and the potential to exploit and abuse that power.

Consent is crucial because sex without consent isn't sex; it's rape. Consent isn't a chore, it should be something that is a part of our culture so every sexual encounter is a consensual, positive and healthy one. And I think we should all make an effort, whether that's by educating others or having good consent practices in our own sex lives.

Alcohol and Sex

I know, technically, this book is aimed at readers of 14+, and the legal age to buy alcohol in the UK is 18. But in Western culture sex and alcohol often go hand in hand, so I think it's important to talk about this. My first-ever one-night stand happened at a house party and, at the point of writing this, the last time I had sex was after a night out, so I can't sit here and pretend to be a perfect role model. But according to the law, someone who is 'intoxicated' cannot consent to sex. By this standard they may be vomiting, unable to stand up, unable to string sentences or words together properly or falling in and out of consciousness. Anyone in that state cannot consent to sex and if you have sex with someone in that state, it is not sex, it's rape. But what about the place in between one drink and drunk? A lot of sex happens in this tipsy, flirty, boozy area and it's important to know how the effects of alcohol on your body and mind can alter your sexual decisions and behaviour.

Most of this information is provided from Sexplanations, a YouTube channel dedicated to sex and relationships education, which is hosted by my dear friend, Dr. Lindsey Doe. Thank you Lindsey and Sexplanations for all your informative and interesting videos, I know they've taught me so much. The first thing to remember is that alcohol affects everyone differently. It depends what kind of alcohol, how much you drink, how much water you've had, how much food is in your stomach, body weight, hormones, age, medications and general health. Rule of thumb: if you're going out drinking, make sure you've eaten a good meal beforehand and that you drink lots of water throughout the evening. You'll still have a good time but you're less likely to get uncontrollably drunk, and you may survive a hangover the next day.

A lot of people have sex when or after they've been drinking so there have to be some good things about it. Alcohol lowers your inhibitions and can give you a bit of 'Dutch courage' which in turn can give you the confidence to say what you really want sexually, truly express yourself and maybe also allow you to try new things. It can be a great tool for helping you to explore your sexuality. Alcohol can give you that warm, fuzzy, relaxed feeling so you worry less about what other people think of you, and can also make you feel turned on, especially bio-sex females. And I can back this up from personal experience. Public spaces where alcohol is consumed can facilitate an environment of sharing, bonding, flirting, and kissing in bars and clubs is usually very acceptable. Yay alcohol!

But now on to the bad ...

Alcohol is a depressant, which means that it slows down the messages from your brain to the different parts of your body, and your body functions. A lot of these functions are the ones used during sex, so it can be difficult to get an erection or to reach orgasm. Alcohol causes dehydration, which can mean dryness in the vagina. People also often talk about 'beer goggles' meaning that alcohol can give you a false sense of who you are attracted to. It's always good to know if you like someone when you're sober. Drunk sex can cause injuries because it's messy, you're a bit all over the place, your reflexes are slow and your brain may not even register pain. This is why, when going out in the cold, we call alcohol a 'beer blanket'. Your body is still cold, but your brain just can't feel it. Not great ... And a really bad thing about alcohol and sex is that often condoms are forgotten about or not put on properly which can lead to the spread of STIs or unplanned pregnancies. There are also more extreme medical and sexual complications that can be caused by long-term alcohol usage. And then there are all the personal relationship problems that can arise from drinking too much alcohol, such as violence, lying, cheating, heartbreak, and low self-esteem.

Also remember that drinking alcohol is not an invitation for sex and it does not excuse sexual assault or rape. You are still 100 per cent accountable for your actions when you're drinking and if someone is extremely drunk, do not lay a hand on them. Keep them safe, do not take advantage. Their drunkenness is not an invitation.

So can you drink alcohol and have sex? Well that depends on all those things mentioned earlier like the type and quantity of alcohol, your weight, your health, etc. Some people drink and have sex, some people drink, sober up and then have sex. In an ideal world, every sexual encounter would be a sober one (it feels better) to avoid any confusion or mishaps, but we live in a culture where alcohol-fuelled sexual experiences are quite common.

There's nothing wrong with having sex after a few drinks, but it's important to be aware of the effects of alcohol on your body and how it can affect your sexual experiences.

Rikki Poynter on Consent and Deafness:

My name is Rikki Poynter and I'm a deaf YouTuber, activist, news writer, and public speaker. I've also been in a relationship with a hearing man for over a year, and we have sex.

Wait, deaf people have sex?

Hearing people have many misconceptions about deaf people and one of them involves sex. In my Sh*t Hearing People Say video, one of the questions I mentioned was something along the lines of, 'How do deaf people have sex?' Sometimes, hearing people don't even ask the question, they assume that deaf people simply can't have sex.

But that's not true. Deaf people can and do have sex. Now, let's talk about consent and being in a deaf-hearing relationship. Because one person can't hear [well], it's very easy to get mixed-up signals. If the deaf person is oral, so can vocalise, (I grew up mainstream/oral, so I can say this from personal experience), they're not going to hear everything that is being said, especially in the dark. During more PG related activities, darkness is a deaf person's enemy, so it's safe to say that extra caution needs to be taken during sexual activity. This is where communication can get a bit tricky, because deaf people need light to see and even hear language if they have residual hearing. I have residual hearing, but I need to be in an area where there is perfect lighting because I have to rely on lip reading as well as hearing to match up the sounds as much as possible.

But you know what? I like having sex in the dark. I'm not a huge fan of having sex with the lights on. Why? It's just the way my brain works. Maybe it's because I'm still sort of a newbie when it comes to sex. (My boyfriend and I are in a long-distance relationship, so I'm not having sex on a daily basis.)

However, I don't like the possibility of my sexual partner getting in and out of bed every minute or two to turn on his iPhone, my iPad, or any electronic advice to type an 'Are you sure?' message, or to turn on the light to try to communicate with me. Yes, yes, consent is important, but if I know what I want, somebody getting in and out of bed constantly is going to get me out of the mood very fast. Thankfully, we can avoid that because he knows very basic ASL (American Sign

Language) and we can tactile ASL our way through our shenanigans. But what happens if you don't know any sign language? Here are a few other ways to communicate and get proper consent. The most important and obvious thing is to discuss your boundaries ahead of time. Talk about what you enjoy, what you don't enjoy, and what you might be apprehensive about but would be willing to try under the right circumstances.

The second thing is to learn some basic sign language, although keep in mind that, just as spoken languages vary from country to country, sign language does too. And while the United States, England and Australia all speak English, their sign languages are not the same. In Hannah's case, she would learn British Sign Language if her partner was also British. Since I live in the United States, I use American Sign Language. Even if the deaf person in the relationship is oral, it would be beneficial for both parties to learn the most basic signs such as 'yes', 'no', 'I want this', 'I don't want this', etc.

A very simple way to ask your deaf partner if they are OK with penetration is simply to hold a condom and wait for them to nod or shake their head. If it's too dark to see, *you could put the condom package in your partner's hand and wait for an answer.*

So, there you have it. Hopefully, this will help you navigate any deaf/hearing relationships you might have in the future.

Rikki Poynter (@rikkipoynter) is a 25-year-old YouTuber and activist who is also deaf. She creates videos that advocate for closed captioning and deaf and disability rights, social issues, and lifestyle and pop culture.

Consent
and the Law

This information has been provided by The Schools Consent Project, a group of volunteer lawyers and law students who do workshops in secondary schools around the UK teaching 11–18 year olds about consent.

In the UK, the general age of consent is 16. But there are some different age limits for things you may not be aware of:

Under 13, all sexual activity is illegal. Regardless of whether or not they consented, sex with someone under 13 is automatically 'statutory rape.'

Under 16, sexual activity is still illegal but if both people have consented and they are close in age then prosecution is unlikely.

Under 18, sexual activity is legal unless one person is in a position of trust (i.e. a teacher, carer, doctor, priest, social worker).

Kate Parker, who is a criminal barrister, knows all about consent and the law and how it practically works out in the courtroom. So I asked her to impart some of her wisdom.

Kate Parker *on Consent*

Consent is the bedrock of any sexual interaction, in that it separates a willing and (hopefully) enjoyable act from a crime.

To be convicted of any sex crime – whether that's sexual assault, oral rape, vaginal rape, etc – a jury will have to be satisfied that (a) the victim did not consent and that (b) the defendant did not reasonably believe that the victim consented. The test is two-pronged because no one is a mind reader. Two people have consensual sex. It cannot be right that if one person turns around at a later date and says that they weren't consenting, the other person is convicted of rape. That person's belief in their partner's consent is just as important.

In sex cases, the prosecution is in a funny position because they have to prove the *absence* of something (consent). Since most sex crimes happen behind closed doors, there don't tend to be independent eyewitnesses or CCTV. The prosecution will point to surrounding evidence such as injuries to the victim (bruising to the wrists, damage to the genital area, etc), the nature of any text/social media contact between the two immediately before and after the incident, when and how the complaint came to light and any inconsistencies in the defendant's account (i.e. if their explanation in a police interview is different to their explanation given in the witness box). Ultimately, these cases rest on which version of events the jury finds more believable.

So what does 'consent' actually mean in law?

The Sexual Offences Act 2003 (the main law which governs sex crime) doesn't give much guidance short of to say that a person consents if he or she 'agrees by choice, and has the freedom and capacity to make that choice'. If someone is unconscious at the time or made to fear violence if they do not comply, there is plainly no freedom of choice. Equally, where someone is not in a position to consent owing to, for example, severe intoxication, there is no capacity to consent. It is important to note that alcohol alone doesn't invalidate consent: people of course still have consensual sex whilst tipsy! It is only when someone is so drunk that they are unable to stand or articulate words, or keeps passing out, that any jury will have serious doubts about their capacity. There is no fixed amount of alcohol beyond which capacity to consent vanishes. Everyone processes alcohol differently, and all sorts of variables (diet, size, medication, usual drinking habits, whether drinks were mixed or not) will impact on an individual's level of intoxication and their capacity to consent.

Given what you now know about the legal side of consent, I've written out a couple of scenarios below. Read them through, and work out if you think consent has been given or not. My own answer and explanation is underneath.

Scenario 1

Casey and Liz went out for three years, during which time they had regular, consensual sex. A few months after they break up, Liz sees Casey at a bar in a club wearing a short skirt. She approaches Casey from behind, runs her hand up her legs, and slips her fingers into Casey's underwear. Liz doesn't understand why Casey is upset and angry.

Answer

There is no consent here. This sex act is done to Casey as opposed to something she chooses to participate in. Liz has made the mistake of assuming that consent to sexual activity once means consent to sexual activity always. It's important to remember that consent – whether spoken or not – has to be clearly given on each separate occasion.

Scenario 2

Josh is Adam's boss. He is 10 years older than Adam and is in charge of promotions at their firm. Adam is desperate to get on in the firm: he is the only breadwinner in his family, and – if promoted – the increased salary will significantly impact their quality of life. After a couple of drinks at the office party, Josh comes on to Adam. He implies that, if Adam sleeps with him, he will ensure he is next in line to be promoted. Adam does not want to have sex with Josh but decides to do so anyway.

Answer

This one turns on whether Adam has the 'freedom' to consent. My view is that he does, in that he made a conscious decision to agree to have sex with Josh with a particular outcome in mind. It may be a bad or difficult or distasteful decision (and is certainly terrible behaviour from Josh), but the law isn't there to rewrite those sorts of decisions: it is to protect citizens when they are forced into something without choice.

Scenario 3

Azi and Dan are in a relationship. As part of their foreplay before sex, they enjoy pretending to put up resistance. Azi normally runs around the room shouting 'no' before being 'captured' by Dan, who lifts her over his shoulder and takes her to the bed. One evening, Azi genuinely doesn't feel like sex. She keeps saying 'no', but Dan assumes it is all part of the foreplay and has sex with her anyway.

Answer

This one is difficult. On the face of it, it looks as though Dan reasonably believed Azi was consenting (and, remember, for a conviction the prosecution have to prove that not only was there no consent but that there was no reasonable belief in consent). However, the reasonableness of this belief will depend on Azi's behaviour. If, for example, she was saying 'no' whilst cowering in the corner of the room and crying, whereas she is normally on her feet and energetic and laughing, the jury may be satisfied that Dan could not have reasonably believed in Azi's consent.

Kate Parker (@SCPLondon) is a criminal barrister practising at 5 Paper Buildings, and the Founder and Director of the Schools Consent Project, an organisation which sends lawyers and law students into schools to teach 11–18 year olds the legal definition of consent and key sexual offences.

So there's a legal definition of 'consent', but what does the law say about rape?

The legal definition of rape is that a man intentionally penetrates someone's vagina/anus/mouth with his penis. Anyone can be a victim of rape regardless of gender but a woman cannot legally rape someone. However, women can be found guilty of another crime, 'assault by penetration', which carries the same sentence as rape – life. The reason the law is like this is to reflect the power dynamic of rape, which is that men are more likely to be perpetrators.

This definition confused me for some time, because what about trans people? Some trans men don't have a penis and some trans women do so how does the law affect them? I asked Kate, and of course she had an answer for me:

> 'Rape has to involve 'penile penetration' (vaginal/anal/oral) whereas assault by penetration involves penetration by a body part (other than a penis) or object. Under section 79(3) of the Sexual Offences Act 2003, the word 'penile' includes surgically constructed penises. So, for example, a trans man who has non-consensual sex with someone using a strap-on would be guilty of assault by penetration. However, a trans man who has non-consensual sex with someone using his surgically constructed penis would be guilty of rape'.

Rape: Myth vs Reality

Myth 1

Most rapes occur in dark alleyways at night-time, and are committed by random strangers, so the best way to stop rape is to not go out alone at night.

Fact 1

The reality is that only around 10 per cent of rapes are committed by strangers. Most rapes are committed by someone who is known to the victim/survivor· and often by someone they have previously trusted, such as a friend, colleague, family member, neighbour, partner or ex-partner. People are more likely to be raped at home by someone they know than by a stranger in a dark alley – we shouldn't use the fear of rape to control people's behaviour and movements, or restrict their freedoms.

Myth 2

Only young, attractive women who wear revealing clothes and are flirtatious are raped.

Fact 2

What someone is wearing, how they look and how they behave is irrelevant – no one ever 'asks for' rape. It is an act of sexual violence and control, there is no excuse for rape and it is never the victim/survivor's fault. People of all ages, appearances, backgrounds, genders, and sexualities are raped, and the only person responsible is the perpetrator.

Myth 3

Women sometimes play 'hard to get', and say 'no' when they really mean 'yes'.

Fact 3

When someone says 'no' to sex, that means no. Everyone has the right to say 'no' and to change their mind at any point. Even if you are lying naked next to someone, you can still say 'no'. Sex is not a challenge or a prize; we must respect the wishes of our sexual partners and believe what they tell us about what they do and don't want.

Myth 4

If you've had sex with a person before, you don't need their consent to do it again.

Fact 4

Consent must be given every time people have sex, regardless of whether they have had sex before. Every. Single. Time.

Myth 5

Alcohol and drugs can turn people into rapists.

Fact 5

Alcohol and drugs are never the cause of rape or sexual assault. It is the fault of the person committing the crime, not the drugs and/or alcohol. Substances don't turn people into rapists or justify sexual violence.

Myth 6

Someone who has drunk a lot of alcohol or taken a lot of drugs can't complain if they are raped.

Fact 6

Nobody, sober or not, deserves to be raped. According to the law, consent can only be given if the person consenting has the capacity to do so. If someone is unconscious or incapacitated by alcohol or drugs then they cannot give consent, and having sex with someone in this state is rape.

Fact 8

There is no typical rapist. People from every different kind of background commit sexual violence.

Myth 7

Rape is only rape if physical force is used, and injuries are caused.

Fact 7

Just because someone doesn't have visible injuries doesn't mean they haven't been raped. Rapists sometimes use weapons or threats of violence to avoid a struggle, or take advantage of someone who cannot fight back. A common reaction to traumatic situations, in addition to the 'fight or flight' response, is to freeze. Some rape victims find themselves unable to move or speak because of fear and shock.

Myth 9

Men cannot help themselves; once they are aroused, they have to have sex.

Fact 9

Men can easily control their sexual urges. And rape is not about being sexually satisfied; it is an act of violence.

Myth 10

People lie about being raped because they want attention or they regret having sex with someone.

Fact 10

The amount of media focus on false rape allegations is disproportionate to the truth, and it just adds to the perception

---

Myth 8

Men of certain races and backgrounds are more likely to be rapists.

that lying about rape is common. False allegations of rape are very rare, in fact most survivors choose not to report it to the police. This can be for many reasons, but one is the fear of not being believed.

Myth 11

People who were sexually abused as children are likely to become abusers themselves.

Fact 11

Excusing or explaining sexually violent behaviour because someone may have been abused in the past is harmful and unhelpful to survivors of childhood abuse, the vast majority of whom will never be perpetrators of sexual violence.

Myth 12

Men can't get raped and women can't commit sexual assault.

Fact 12

Anyone can be a victim of rape or sexual assault. Whilst the majority of sexual assaults and rapes are committed by men against women, a small number of women do perpetrate sexual violence. Men can also be raped, and the impact of this is no less devastating than for women.

What to do
if you are a victim of
rape or sexual assault

Firstly, whatever you are feeling, please try to remember that it is not your fault, you didn't 'ask for it' and your behaviour or actions don't mean that you are to blame for what happened to you. Please also try to remember that you are not alone. It may seem that way, like you can't tell anyone and that no one will understand, but there are people out there who will listen and can help.

Secondly, however you choose to respond to the situation is completely up to you. There is no right or wrong way to react when something like this happens, just do what you can to make yourself feel better and safer. As much as I believe it's important for victims to come forward, only do that if you feel comfortable.

Here are some things you can do to access both formal and informal support:

Tell someone

A friend or family member.

Go to A&E

You may be in need of medical attention. Also, if you decide to go to the police and you seek medical attention soon afterwards (and before you've showered) then this can be used as evidence and will help your case. That said, it is very normal for victims to want to shower immediately afterwards, and for obvious reasons not to want strangers examining their body after a traumatic experience.

Tell the police

Only around 15 per cent of people who experience sexual violence report it to the police. That is so low. Many people don't go to police because of the low conviction rate, and a fear of not being believed. Despite the fear, and these statistics, I would really encourage you to file a report with the police if you can ...

Talk to a professional

A doctor, counsellor, or therapist. There is no shame in seeking help to deal with the experience and to come to terms with what happened.

Go online

There are so many places there where you can seek support, whether that's from people who have gone through a similar thing to you, or professionals. If you feel like you can't talk to anyone in person, there are loads of great resources that can help you, too. A lot of these websites will also have phone numbers so you can speak to someone directly.

There is a list of helpful websites, phone numbers and organisations at the end of this book. So, in summary:

1) **Make sure you get consent and that the person consenting has the freedom and capacity to make that choice.**

2) **If you're unsure at any point, just ask.**

Chapter 6

masturbation

Self-love

'I love me!
Gonna love myself, no,
*I don't need anybody else.'**

– Hailee Steinfeld

Masturbation, self-pleasure, me time, busting one out ... the euphemisms are endless, and so are the benefits to spending a little time looking out for your own sexual pleasure. Masturbation is a thing that almost everyone does and no one talks about, but I'm here to break that silence. So let's smash it. Masturbation is not a dirty, gross, selfish, loveless act. We talk about self-care for our minds: breathing, taking time off work and socialising, pampering yourself, relaxing, switching off from the Internet. Well masturbation is self-care for down there and everywhere else – it's truly magical. Whatever you want to call it, masturbation is all about *your* experience: your pleasure, your fantasies and your unique sexuality. It's about the exploration of your body and what makes you tick physically and mentally – it is completely normal and there are loads of benefits to it. The main one being that it feels soooo good! Whether you orgasm or not, the feelings of sexual arousal and pleasure are wonderful and you should cherish them. I say this about orgasm because some people

---

* From the song Love Myself by Mattias Larsson, Robin Fredriksson, Oscar Holter, Julia Michaels, Hailee Steinfeld and Justin Tranter.

see masturbation as a way to reach this end goal and sometimes that's fine, sometimes you just need that release. But sometimes, that focus on trying to orgasm makes having an orgasm less likely. So it's about enjoying the pleasure in the moment, as it's happening. Being in the present and focusing on the pleasure you're experiencing make masturbation a fantastic way to relieve stress. Whatever's worrying you, masturbation is a great way to de-stress and just focus on yourself for a minute, or two minutes, or an hour. Don't ask how but I had an orgasm on a plane once. Yep. Now, I am not a confident flyer – I get panic attacks during turbulence – but for this flight I was so calm and relaxed. The prospect of potentially falling out of the sky didn't cross my mind at all. Another thing masturbation is great for – sleep! We all know the cliché that men fall asleep after sex, well it's kind of true, and it works for women too. The hormones we release after an orgasm can help to knock us out and to sleep much better (not going to lie, I've definitely used this technique to fight off jet lag before).

Masturbating is a great way to get to know your body and your own sexual pleasure: what you like, what you don't like, what kinds of fantasies turn you on, what types of touches and movements you like.

It's a safe place to experiment with your pleasure. And getting to know your body like that is so empowering. Self-pleasure makes people happier, more confident and feel better about their body. Masturbation increases body positivity? You don't have to ask me twice, I am on board. Next stop: masturbation station! Also, the more you know about your own pleasure, the better the sex you'll have with someone else because you can communicate what feels good to you. Some people say that when you get into a relationship sex replaces masturbation, or that if you masturbate when you're in a relationship then that takes away from partnered sex. But this just isn't true.

Masturbation adds to sex and sex adds to masturbation. You could even try masturbating together. A common thing to happen, though, especially if you have a vagina, is that even if your partner is doing exactly the same thing that you do when you masturbate, it might take longer for you to reach orgasm or it might not happen at all. And don't worry, this is completely normal – it doesn't mean you're broken, that you're not into your partner or that they have bad technique. It's just something that our bodies do.

Sometimes during masturbation, especially if it's vaginal, you might feel like you need to pee. This is because your bladder is really quite close to everything, but it's more likely you're going to orgasm or ejaculate. I used to worry about this a lot, particularly during sex, so much so that I'd have to stop because I was scared I was going to wet myself. It's unlikely to happen, but if you are still worried then pee before you have sex or masturbate, put a towel down or play in the bath or shower. And don't forget to breathe, relax and let go. Some people like to use sex toys like vibrators, dildos, anal beads or butt plugs, etc, when they masturbate. Just make sure that the material they are made out of is body-safe and you clean them properly afterwards. Materials that we currently know are safe to go near your genitals are 100 per cent silicone and glass, and make sure they are also phthalate-free. If you are unsure then put a condom on them. Another great thing about masturbation is that it's safe – you can't get pregnant or catch STIs.

As much as I love masturbation, and telling people how good for them it is, there is such a thing as 'too much'. But everyone is different so it varies from person to person. If you are asking yourself, 'do I masturbate too much?' you might want to check your intentions when you masturbate and the context you do it in. Is it stopping you from doing other things in your life? We shouldn't judge people for how much or how little they masturbate but if you think it's a problem or it's becoming painful then you should speak to your doctor. At the other end of the spectrum are people who have no interest in masturbation. Maybe you're asexual (although some asexual people do masturbate), maybe it doesn't feel good to you or maybe there's a psychological barrier preventing you from enjoying it. If something doesn't feel right then you don't have to do it – it's your body. But if you do want to enjoy masturbation and for whatever reason you can't, it might be worth talking to a doctor.

One thing that I wish I'd been taught about masturbation when I was younger is that female masturbation does not equal fingering. Some people do masturbate vaginally but for most the clitoris is the main pleasure spot.

Out of all the organs of the human body (male or female), the clitoris is the only one whose sole purpose is for pleasure! How incredible is that?! That is literally all it is there for, so use it.

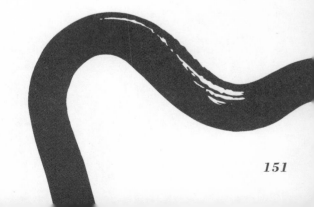

How I discovered masturbation

I was very late to the party. It didn't have my first orgasm until I was 20 and then it took another two years until someone other than myself could also give me an orgasm. And from the time I'm writing this I just had my second orgasm during penetrative sex last week. The first one was five or six months ago. It's a journey, guys.

So what's the deal? Why was I so late to the party? Was I taking too long picking an outfit or doing my hair or makeup? Well no, for years I actually thought the party was disgusting. (By party I mean masturbation, by the way.) As a teenager, I was completely grossed out by the idea of touching myself 'down there'. To be honest, I really can't pinpoint anything in my childhood or adolescence that put me off it except that no one talked about it. It wasn't even presented as an option to me. I knew it existed because I read *Cosmopolitan* but it felt like something reserved for women in their 20s and 30s, one of those 'you'll find out when you're older' things. I had no interest in it.

The boys in my school talked about their penises all the time. I was friends with a lot of guys who would tell me about their recent 'session' and I remember once being in a room with a bunch of guys who were comparing how far their semen could reach when they ejaculated. I look back on this and I can't remember feeling weird about it, I just laughed along because the idea of boys self-pleasuring was completely normal. But not for those of us with vaginas. Since opening up more about masturbation, I asked some of my friends from school when they first started doing it and it's like 12, 13, 14 years old. I was standing there thinking 'WHY DID NO ONE TELL ME ABOUT THIS?'

How did everyone else know about the world's best-kept secret except me? Why did it take me 20 years to figure this out?

I did try to finger myself once when I was 13. That is a horrible sentence that I never expected to write, ever. Finger. I'd been talking to a boy from school who I really liked on MSN, we were in a strange secret relationship which we won't go into here, but it was basically because he was my best friend's brother. We said that we wanted to 'do stuff' together, I can't remember the exact terms I used at 13 but I imagine they were something like 'toss off' and 'finger'. I shudder. This was all very new to me, I'd never gone that far with a boy before and I didn't know what to expect or what it would be like for him. So one evening in the bath I put one of my fingers inside my vagina to see what it would feel like. It was warm and squishy, I didn't particularly like it and I got no pleasure from the experience. So I don't think that counts as the first time I tried to masturbate.

As I got older and was less grossed out by the idea of self-pleasure, and growing more and more painfully aware about the lack of orgasms in my sex life, I became increasingly frustrated. Even though I knew it was normal for some women, I just couldn't let it go. At this point I'd started making sex education videos on YouTube and I felt like such a fraud. I was very honest with my sexual partners and I can proudly say that I have never faked an orgasm. People are always shocked when I tell them that but I don't see the point in lying because then the other person will never truly learn how to please you. Some people I slept with wanted to take on making me orgasm as their personal mission, but that only made me feel more anxious because of the pressure, which then made it less likely to happen.

When it finally did happen, it was just me. Alone, all the time in the world, not rushed, relaxed, in the comfort of my home with an open incognito window of porn and a vibrator. I wasn't expecting anything to happen, instead of focusing on this end goal I just tried to enjoy the pleasure in the moment as it was happening (and also the porn I was watching). Not worrying about whether or not I was going to cum led to my first orgasm. I was practising mindfulness before I even learnt about it. People always told me that you know when you have an orgasm and oh boy did I know. I immediately called the guy I was seeing at the time and excitedly told him that I'd had an orgasm. He wasn't as enthusiastic as I was hoping but it didn't matter because I was happy as hell.

Oh my god, the dopamine!

Now I am a big fan of female masturbation and not grossed out by it at all. And because I was late to the party, I feel like I've got a lot of catching up to do. To be honest, just writing this has got my mind wandering ...

How I masturbate

E veryone's pleasure is different and there's no right or wrong way to masturbate: lying down, standing up, in the shower, with toys, with your imagination, in the dark, with candles ... it's good to experiment but everyone has their go-to ritual so I asked some of my friends to share with me how their self-pleasure sessions usually go down.

When I masturbate I like to create some mood lighting. I close the curtains, turn the main lights off and turn my lamps and fairy lights on. I prefer there to be no distracting sounds so it's usually when I'm home alone or in the evening after my housemates have gone to bed. I lay a towel down on my bed because sometimes a little extra fluid comes out. Sometimes I like to be naked and other times I like to just have a t-shirt on. I like to switch it up between using a small vibrator and my hands because I don't want my pleasure to become dependent on a device – I like to know that I've still got it. I used to watch porn but now my imagination is all I need and it is wonderful. Afterwards, I clean the vibrator if I used one, put it back in my cupboard, throw the towel on the ground, turn off the lights, and go to sleep.

Tools: never fingers. I always use a bullet and occasionally a phallic vibrator when I haven't had sex in a while.

How to set the mood: I have to watch chat shows, I'm not aroused by them, but they're funny and easy to watch and they make me happy. I'm not sure why I don't like porn or why I don't masturbate with anything else on, but that's just how it is I guess. Sometimes I have to do it in the bath/shower (no water) because I have a tendency to squirt. But fingers don't really do anything for me – it's all about the clitoris.

If I'm just trying to tire myself out to get to sleep I have my phone with erotic fiction in one hand and read for a bit until I get going then whack it out. If I've got the house to myself, I'll take my time with the vibrator.

I'll usually be thinking of someone I know or an interaction I had that day that got me turned on, but I'll use porn as an added stimulant – for me it's the extra sounds that help, rather than the imagery. Almost always lying down, a couple of pillows to keep my upper body a bit elevated. I like to be naked, as it's easier to clean up when there aren't any clothes involved, but depending on what's to hand I'll masturbate into a tissue or (if I'm feeling fancy!) a condom. I very rarely use lubricant, and I don't have any toys – I keep thinking I'd like to but never get round to investing. I'm a right-hander, usually starting slow, and mainly massage the top of the shaft rather than large strokes. Once there's pre-cum I'll mix the larger massaging strokes with fingertips at the sensitive point between the head and the shaft.

I live with my boyfriend and he isn't very good at pleasuring me. He's lazy. So I wait until I'm home alone and I go up to our bedroom, lock the door and get my vibrator. As I write this I'm thinking about how I need to replace those batteries. It's an Ann Summers one that probably needs updating but it has five settings and it feels so nice. I put a towel on top of the bed and close the blinds. I do put my bedside light on because I still want to be able to see myself. I don't use porn, I used to, but I ended up feeling so awful half-way through because most of it is very degrading to women. Until I see porn for women made by women where women are genuinely enjoying themselves I very much doubt I'll use porn to masturbate. I use my imagination, which is king, let's be honest. I can take myself anywhere with anyone. Mostly I think of this guy I had amazing sex with in the past. Out-of-this-world, outrageous sex. He's so generous, and would spend a long time giving oral. I imagine him doing it to me as I use my vibrator. It's the ultimate turn-on because it's personal. I can't quite come on board with people who think of celebs whilst they masturbate. My fantasies are much closer to home and if I ever use my L'Occitane almond oil, the smell of it reminds me of the hottest massage I ever had (obviously from him). I masturbate lying on my back, knees up, eyes closed and let the vibrator do the work. After a while I turn over and lay down flat on my stomach with the vibrator underneath me for a more intense sensation as the weight of my body makes the vibrations stronger. Often my legs start shaking and my vagina has its own pulse going on and I've worked up a bit of a sweat. It's like that moment during sex where you sort of want it to stop but you don't at the same time. Finally I surrender myself, switch off the vibrator and just lie there for a bit. It's usually at that point where I have revelations like 'I should start doing online food shopping'. Then I laugh to myself. I used to get post-wank guilt (probably because I grew up in a religious family) but now I just put all my tools away and crack on with my day.

Left-handed even though I'm right-handed.
Always stood up, literally always. Usually
think about someone I know. Quite often
play music.

I usually use a bullet, at night-time when
I go to bed, and dream of situations that
definitely would never happen (i.e. Zac
Efron sneaking me off at a club night).

Chapter 7

porn

We can't ignore porn. And we can't just say, 'don't watch it' because at some point in their lives, most people will. It's unrealistic to try and stop young people from watching porn, or to ban it. What is realistic is to acknowledge some of the problems with porn and to offer a counter-narrative to it. A lot of young people learn about sex and relationships from what they see in porn and, because of the lack of decent sex and relationship education in schools, this can have some devastating effects. It's not that all porn is evil, but if we deny young people the tools to think critically about porn, healthy relationships and body image then it might as well be. Porn can give people a lot of false expectations about sex and bodies that can be harmful to them and their partners. So here's your counter-narrative. I'm not shaming you for watching porn; I sometimes indulge myself, too. But here's the truth ...

Porn myth busting

Penises and vaginas and boobs, oh my ...

There is a typical porn star image – they have big dicks, tiny vulvas and big perky boobs. For young people who watch porn, those genitals are often the only genitals other than their own that they see. This creates a lot of anxiety around the way their own bodies look. Penis too small, labia too big, too much hair, boobs too small, boobs too saggy. You may watch porn and think, 'mine doesn't look like that, does that mean I'm not normal?' Noooooo! You are normal. The reality is that most penises aren't *that* big, the average length of an erect penis in the UK is 5.5 inches. Vulvas come in all shapes, sizes and colours, and the same with boobs and nipples. Some porn stars have had plastic surgery, and not just on their breasts. An operation called a labiaplasty reduces the size of the labia minora (the flaps of skin on either side of the vaginal opening), and that's the reason that many porn stars' vulvas can often look tiny and tucked – it's surgery. Most porn stars also have little or no hair and so people watching think that's what their body is supposed to look like, or expect their partner to be hairless. Ultimately, though, it's your body so you do what you want with it. Most women have some hair. It's unfortunate that for so many young people, the only bodies they see are the ones in porn or the toned and primped bodies of celebrities in the media. Not everyone looks like that, in fact, most people don't! Bodies come in all shapes and sizes, and so do penises and vaginas.

Just because you don't have the body of a porn star does not mean you're ugly or unsexy.

Performance

There are many things about the sexual performance of people in porn that are simply unrealistic when it comes to 'real sex.' First of all, in porn it seems like the man can keep his massive erection forever, and last a really long time before he ejaculates. Secondly, women have really intense orgasms all the time from penetration alone, and partners always cum at the same time. Thirdly, sex is only good if you can do all these crazy positions, and people moan and groan and fling their hair around in order to show pleasure. If you watch a lot of porn before you have sex for the first time, or you're slightly inexperienced, then this may seem really intimidating. It might feel like you're not good enough because you usually cum within two minutes, or you don't cum at all. Maybe it makes you feel self-conscious and stupid doing all the moaning and screaming, or you can't for the life of you imagine how your body is going to get into that position. Remember, porn is entertainment. It's not real. These actors are professionals. If you think of sex as a sport then porn is the Olympics – athletes participating in feats of endurance, flexibility and orgasm. But for the rest of us, who aren't sexual athletes, playing sport can still be super-fun and rewarding. When I'm playing tennis I'm not thinking, 'this is no fun because I'll never be as good as Serena Williams.' No. I'm thinking, 'hey, I'm having a really good time and I'm playing my best and my partner and I got a really good rally going just then!' Sex is about the connection between people, so if you're in tune with each other then it's going to be good no matter what kind of sex you have. To further bust this anxiety-ridden sex performance myth, here are some facts:

> *Different studies will give you different answers about how long on average it takes men to ejaculate during intercourse.*

But remember, this is just during intercourse and doesn't include many of the other fun acts involved in sex. Some say the average is about five minutes and others say anywhere between one minute and 20 minutes. So there's no right or wrong amount of time you're supposed to last, what's right is what feels good for you and your partner. If you are worried that you are cumming too soon or taking too long then try talking to your doctor, or another healthcare professional.

This next piece of information has been so important to me personally in feeling normal about my body – most women cannot orgasm from penetration alone. We need some external stimulation too! And even clitoral stimulation during penetrative sex can be hard to master. So don't worry, there's nothing wrong with you if this is the case. Also, cumming at the same time? Great if it works for you and your partner, but pretty sure I will never master this.

Women are objects to play with

The way women are treated is my main issue with porn. The fact that a lot of young people are watching this and thinking that it is normal. And the damaging effect that has on young people and how they view healthy sexual relationships. The majority of mainstream straight porn is made by men and for men. This means it's about male pleasure and the woman in porn is just a body whose function is to give pleasure to the man. A lot of the porn I've seen isn't sexy at all, and the woman either looks like she's faking it or in physical pain. Female pleasure is irrelevant – how many blowjobs do I have to watch before I see some appealing cunnilingus? Fake lesbian oral sex doesn't count either, because that's still made for men to watch and get themselves off. Women have very little agency or body autonomy in porn; they are portrayed as objects that sex happens to rather than being active partners in the experience. I shouldn't have to explain how and why this is harmful, but in a world where the majority of . rapes and sexual assaults are committed by men against women, the treatment of women in porn feeds into the idea that men are sexually dominant and entitled to a woman's body whenever they want it. This is a completely unhealthy idea that doesn't stem only from porn, but porn is a big culprit in perpetuating it. In real life and in real sex, partners are equal. Pleasure is shared and there is only a cum shot to the face at the end if the other person has explicitly consented to it.

All porn stars have STIs

This comes from a common myth, which is that only sexually promiscuous people get STIs. Wrong. And when it comes to porn stars, the truth is the exact opposite, they actually have fewer STIs than the general public. Whether they use condoms or not depends on the production and the preference of the actors, but porn stars regularly get tested for STIs to stop them spreading anything around. Very smart! If only the general public did the same ...

Unrealistic expectations of sex

Another falsehood that porn sex normalises is how hardcore some of it is. This can be anything from hard and fast doggy-style to kinky BDSM (Bondage, Discipline/Dominance, Submission/Sadomasochism). Not everyone is into that kind of sex and porn really isn't the best place to learn about kink and how to do it consensually and safely. The amount of more extreme sex that occurs in porn can give people unrealistic expectations of what 'normal' sex is. Most people's sex lives aren't that hardcore and there's nothing wrong with that. What you shouldn't do is expect your sexual partner to behave in a certain way and be up for anything just because you've seen it in a porn film.

The other part of porn that is completely unrealistic is that the sex always ends when the man ejaculates.

Sex shouldn't be a means to an end, it's an end in itself and the goal-orientated sex we see in a lot of porn grossly underplays the wonderful amazingness of what I like to call a 'sex session'. A 'session' can last minutes or hours. There can be no orgasms or lots of orgasms. There can be breaks in between different activities and perhaps there may not even be any penetration. Straight porn begins with an erection and ends with an ejaculation, but sex doesn't have to be like this. That misses out so much good stuff!

Porn addiction

Porn addiction is a real thing and it can be very damaging. But it isn't something that just happens overnight, it can creep up on you over a long period of time. An addiction to pornography can negatively affect your sex life and your relationships (not just with partners but with friends and family too). Your body can also become desensitised to porn the more you watch it, which means that things that used to turn you on may no longer arouse you, and only more hardcore and extreme porn will work. It may be that porn becomes the only thing you can get aroused by and have an orgasm from. If you're worried about the amount of porn that you consume, if it's affecting your relationships or day-to-day life or if it's the only way you can get aroused, then you should speak to someone about it and get help. As with any addiction, it can be beaten, but you will need support.

Someone I know has previously had an addiction to porn but managed to beat it, and I thought I would let him share his experience with you.

Let's call him Oliver.

Hannah: When did you first start watching porn?

> Oliver: Very young, probably 12 or 13. It's actually quite
> sad for me to think that by the time I'd quit at 25, I'd been
> watching for half my life.

*H: How did your porn addiction develop and when did
you realise that it was a problem?*

> O: It developed after I'd started masturbating. I overheard
> boastful comments in school from more alpha male lads
> in my class about masturbating three/four times a day and
> watching porn. I took it quite literally and began to think
> I should be doing the same. It led me to watch more and
> more porn to get the same effect. I ended up watching
> a lot of hardcore pornography, although by the end I
> settled on watching the same 8/10 videos each time, a bit
> like an alcoholic who only drinks one drink. I've watched
> everything! I'm a cisgender straight man about 1.5 on the
> Kinsey Scale, but I have gone through pretty much all of it.

*H: How did it affect your relationships? (Either with
partners or family/friends)*

> O: It's affected a lot of my relationships but none in my
> family, thank God. My relationships with women became
> more and more detached and I increasingly saw sex as a
> 'sport' or an activity to get good at. I became obsessed
> with making my partners orgasm, to the point of ignoring
> my own sexual pleasure. I've also experienced erectile
> dysfunction to varying degrees, although nothing more
> serious than a bruised ego for a few nights. The biggest
> problem I've faced with arousal addiction, and I cannot
> stress enough the difference between arousal addiction
> and pornography addiction*, is that I've felt completely
> worthless when I've been on dates or nights in and I'm not
> erect all the time. As if it were threatening my masculinity or
> my sexuality. It led to serious depression and undermined

** Arousal addiction is the constant desire to be erect, porn addiction is the constant
desire to watch porn.*

my self-confidence so badly that I'd actively avoid dating or trying to pick up girls on nights out. It was so much easier to go home and masturbate. Why go through the heartache and effort of a relationship? It led me to explore relationships with men, which was enlightening but ultimately I'm not romantically attracted to men and sex with a man, for me, isn't as complete an experience as sex with a woman. When I did have sex, however, I could not achieve orgasm without thinking about porn, no matter how aroused my partner made me. I still struggle with this problem to a small degree. You can see why this made me anxious and depressed.

H: *What did you do to seek help when you realised you were addicted?*

O: I actually brought the subject up with a private psychotherapist but he saw nothing wrong with my activity or my behaviour. This was nearly seven years ago – the effects of pornography were still considered a very new field in psychology. (They still are – because there's 'no one' not watching porn to study for comparison.) I began to realise my anxiety and depression about my constant desire to be aroused were really unhealthy maybe a year before I talked to my psychotherapist, but his reaction was the wrong kind of reassuring. I continued my behaviour until I started to experiment with giving up masturbating as a personal challenge in 2012, and it was great. But I hadn't made the decision to quit fully until I watched a TED talk discussing what happens to your brain and endorphins when you watch porn. In my experience, there isn't a lot of help out there apart from some education on the Internet and the 'no-fap' community**. All Google-friendly and easy to access.

** *An online community that serves as a support group for those who wish to avoid pornography, masturbation or sexual intercourse. The subreddit has more than 200,000 members.*

H: What was your recovery process like?

O: I quit in December 2014. I literally just decided that was it. For ever. I no longer suffer with depression, I'm no longer anxious in my normal day-to-day life, my confidence has gone through the roof. My recovery has been an amazing boost and I'm enjoying my life more than I ever have done. After just two months I found myself turning into this really outgoing person on nights out and I was able to talk to women and be part of the dating game again. Before I quit, I just wouldn't have been interested. Sex is a motivator. What can I say? And sex is actually enjoyable now. What a novelty!

H: Do you watch any porn now?

O: No, no, I do not!

H: Are you anti-porn?

O: I'm certainly advocating for stricter controls on who can enter porn sites and how you can access porn. I'm a pragmatic person. People are all different and I don't want to take away your bukaki videos on a Friday night if that's what you're into. But the human brain isn't meant to consume pornography at the rate we currently are. There's no distinction between porn and actual sex in the brain. None. So if you have the appetite for it, and you know when you've had enough, then good. But if not, then please get help.

H: What advice would you give to a) young people who are discovering porn for the first time and b) someone who may be concerned about their porn consumption?

O: If you're struggling then give it up. The change could be profound. But if you struggle with addiction more than I did then get psychiatric help. My experience might be very different to yours and if you treat this as an addiction, you'll get help as an addict. Join the 'no-fap' community and give a month off porn a go. If that goes well, make it two months. See how far you can get. If you're 13, the Internet is a shitty place. The fact I was watching porn that young scares and saddens me. If you're a young person discovering pornography then I'd advise you to think really critically about what porn says on women as objects and what it could do to your perception of sex. Sex is amazing. Porn isn't sex. Not even close! Before I'd even had my first kiss I had perceptions about how a girl should give me a blowjob (some women aren't going to do that), be able to ride me reverse cowgirl (I've caused damage doing that), be totally OK with anal (most women won't do that). All of these perceptions made me really uncomfortable exploring sex in real life. I'd already explored it alone and now I had to let someone into this weird solo sex sphere I'd created for myself. It really put pressure on my first relationships, which made me unhappy. I didn't think of women as people to have sex with, they were someone to 'do sex to'. That is the most awful sentence I'll ever say/write in my entire life. Porn is actually rubbish. But it looks pretty sweet, doesn't it? Don't worry. It's just your brain tricking you. And you don't have to let it.

Is porn evil?

OK, so we've heard a lot of bad things about porn so far and they certainly aren't to be ignored, but what about the other side? Can porn be a force for good? Is there any 'good' porn out there? I mean, a lot of people watch porn so there must be something appealing about it, right? Well, it can be a great tool for masturbation, it can help you learn about your sexuality and what you do and don't like, and it's entertainment. Sexy entertainment! It can also be a fun thing to watch with your partner, a shared experience to get yourselves going and tease until you can ravish each other. (Is this me trying to write erotic fiction? 'Ravish'? OK Hannah, get a grip.) As with most things, watching porn in moderation can be a fun, harmless thing.

But as I said, if we're watching porn we need to be able to separate it from the reality of sex, otherwise it can become a negative thing. And even though the majority of the free, accessible, mainstream porn is of this gross kind of nature, that doesn't mean there aren't companies out there making all kinds of different porn, even sex-positive feminist porn. Back in June 2016, my friend Melanie Murphy and I got the opportunity to go to Barcelona to meet the erotic film director Erika Lust. We visited the set of her latest short film to see her in action and meet the cast and crew and yes, we watched people have sex. It was incredible. It didn't feel seedy at all and Erika really took care of the actors. It didn't feel like we were watching a 'porno' being filmed either, it felt like we were watching two people having a real sex session, there just happened to be a camera and other people around.

Erika Lust on *Sex-positive Pornography:*

Porn ... What does it mean to you? You've probably seen it on a pop-up advert on the Internet, or on the TV, or in a music video. Sometimes, it's in a subverted form in a fashion advert or magazine, or maybe you've gone looking for it for yourself. Porn is everywhere and it's a huge part of our culture. But what do you often see when you watch mainstream porn? A woman, big-breasted, covered in makeup, ready to give the man what he wants, as a reward for, say, fixing her car? How does that make you feel? If you feel ashamed, it's OK. If you feel aroused, it's OK. If you feel like you can't relate to anything happening on screen, join the club!

For too long, mainstream porn has shown us a very negative, unrealistic and one-sided view of sex. Women are objects of desire, to be won and to give pleasure, but never to receive it. Many positions can only be executed by endurance and Olympic athletes, and the women moan in 'pleasure' as soon as a hand is laid on them, even if it's nowhere near their clitoris. The men, on the other hand, are there as machines to use the women as they please. There's no life, no joy, no love, no real pleasure and an uncertain sense of consent between those involved. It's often fake, unrealistic and outrageous. And trust me – nothing at all like real sex. Does that seem equal and fair to you? But most importantly, does that mean it has to stay the same forever?

Sex-positive porn is a huge movement that you may not know about, and that's where I come in. I am a leading female director of adult cinema. Yes, I film sex for a living. But from a female perspective, where men and women are treated as equals, where both are sexual beings with desires and needs and BOTH receive pleasure. I film sex in the most natural way possible, showing REAL pleasure. Where sex is everything it's supposed to be – fun, passionate, pleasurable, and where consent and equality are paramount. How did I begin filming? When I was younger, I saw porn for the first time at a girls' slumber party after one of my friends found her dad's hidden VHS (this was before DVDs and digital downloads) and decided we should all watch it. I was, of course, excited! The mysterious and exciting world of sex and porn at our fingertips ... but I couldn't help but feel disgust. Yes, I was turned on, we are all animals after all! But overall I could see

that it was tacky, it was ugly, the women did not look like they were enjoying themselves, and the sexual situations were pretty laughable or disgusting.

I've always considered myself free and open-minded, and I've always had this crazy idea that women should enjoy sex as much as men. So years later, I studied political sciences, feminism and sexuality at university in Sweden, and came across a book called Hard Core: Power, Pleasure, and the Frenzy of the Visible, *by Linda Williams. It explained that pornography is a discourse on sexuality and gender, and I thought to myself ' Why is it that this discourse is only in the hands of men?' Isn't that crazy? I was inspired by that book to portray sex the way I see it: beautiful, intelligent, and full of joy; and to portray the desire that can lead to it though stories. A reaction to the negative portrayals of sex and gender in mainstream porn. As you may know, mainstream porn is mostly made by white, heterosexual men who are comfortable dishing out the same, repetitive films and perpetuating often very violent and dangerous images of sex, sexuality and men and women. Why? Because it has always worked for them. But how do you change something you don't like? By getting into it! I am not the only woman doing sex-positive* porn or adult cinema (as I prefer to call it) and our numbers are growing. But we do need more women in porn. We need their perspective as women. We need them in leading roles as directors, producers and scriptwriters, to make explicit films that are sex-positive, so young people can see sex in a light that is real and pleasurable, and where equality and consent are in every part. Right now, I work with a crew that is 90 per cent female, something absolutely weird for the industry.

A year ago I decided to create a crowd-sourced project where people like you and me confess their sex fantasies and I choose two every month to turn into explicit short films where I can bring real sex stories to life. Believe me, there is no resemblance at all to the kind of porn you may be familiar with now. There is a lot of effort put into the casting, the decoration, the clothes, the styling, the music, the script, the photography: all of these are key elements for me. Later, colour correction and post-production are crucial too. My team is as large as that of any indie movie you might see in your local cinema, and we put just as much, if not more, effort into making sure each film presents a positive view of sexuality and sex. I create relatable stories where

desire is born and explicit sex happens. The stories, as in life, are different each time, but my characters always end up having sex for a reason. They are natural characters, diverse in beauty, bodies and personalities, and there is a lot of attention to detail. I am also ethical about the signals I send out with my stories – I make consent clear, I don't show irresponsible scenes or anything to do with coercion, etc.

Regarding the performers, they are the most important part for me. I am attentive to their needs, requests and emotions, and I provide a good working environment with good working conditions and salary. The result? Realistic, fun and very relatable short films. We are sexual beings, so my aim is to make people feel good and confident about their sexuality whatever it is. I create beautiful adult cinema, that aims to inspire positivity about sex and to show that female pleasure matters. That is the most important message.

Erika Lust (@erikalust) is a filmmaker, mother, writer, blogger, owner and founder of Erika Lust Films where she offers an alternative to the mainstream porn industry.

My relationship with porn

As a teenager, I knew that porn existed but I wasn't that curious about it, and the idea of it didn't really appeal to me so I never searched for it online. I also had no idea how to hide my computer history from my parents so didn't want to risk it! Although, I do remember a bunch of my guy friends showing me an infamous video of a penis just spinning around and around (you know the one) when I was about 13, and I was horrified. I don't really remember much about my relationship with porn between 13 and 20, which probably means I completely avoided it. And at 20 I had my first orgasm from masturbation and porn was a very useful stimulant in that experience. I remember opening up an incognito window and searching 'porn for women'. I was too scared of what would appear on my screen if I just searched 'porn'. The extra visible and audible stimulant helped me achieve my first-ever orgasm so I'm actually super-grateful for porn. Without it, it may have taken me way longer to discover this wonderful thing that my body can do. Because it had worked the first time, the next time I tried I watched porn again and then the next time and the next time. I started to discover what I liked (home

videos of swinger parties by the way – it
seems I'm turned on by people who just
love sex). Eventually, though, I learnt
how to use my own fantasies instead
of relying on porn, and I have to say my
imagination is better than most
porn I've seen! Occasionally I
dip back into porn, but nowadays
it's only sex-positive, feminist porn like the
type of films Erika makes. There's a whole
movement of people making this ethical
kind of porn and it's really exciting to me.
So even though I am thankful to porn for
helping me out with my first orgasm, I've
flown the nest and I no longer need it
(except when I want it).

Chapter 8

bodies
and
body image

Bodies are weird right?

They're made of flesh, skin and bone and all these organs that
we can't see but that work all kinds of magic and literally keep
us alive. Can you tell I'm not a doctor? Bodies are a bit mysterious,
but they shouldn't be. Understanding our bodies (especially around
the genital area) and their functions can be empowering and allow us
to gain a sense of control over our bodies. Not knowing what's going
on 'down there', feeling uncertain about some bodily functions and not
knowing who you can talk to about it can be scary. If we haven't been
taught what's what and the purpose of everything, or encouraged to
explore or openly and confidently ask questions, then it's no wonder
that a lot of our bodily functions involving genitals feel shameful
and embarrassing.

When I was 10 I thought I had a penis (and not in a penis-envy way).
Hear me out. I watched a documentary on TV about people who
were intersex. I didn't really understand what it meant, and what
10-year-old me took from it was that some girls could have penises.
I remember being in the bath later that evening and probably for the
first time ever I had a feel around in between my legs to see what

was going on. I didn't really know what anything was. I knew I peed from there, probably had an idea about my vagina, no clue about the clitoris and wait, what's this flap of skin?! Is this my undeveloped penis?! No, it was one of my labia minora flaps. But at the time and for days, maybe even weeks afterwards, I thought I had a penis and I was terrified. I didn't want a penis. I was too scared to tell anyone that I thought I was half-boy. Then I got older and learned about the labia, had a proper look around with a mirror and felt much better.

I realise that this is a very strange example, but it's not far off what a lot of people experience. They discover things in between their legs that no one has told them about and jump to conclusions. Or the opposite, (and this mainly applies to people with vaginas because most of it is hidden away), you don't discover everything and you get to adulthood not knowing what the clitoris is (I met someone at university who didn't know) or that there are three holes. So my advice to you is (in private), get yourself comfortable and have a look in front of a mirror. Have a look around, have a feel around and get to know yourself. You might have some mental barriers about doing this, there's a lot to unlearn about our relationship with our bodies before we can start to have a positive and healthy reaction to our genitals. But take your time, there's no pressure. You're not a prude if it makes you feel uncomfortable at first. Take baby steps, maybe full spreading your legs and poking around is something that you need to build up to. And that's fine. But believe me, it's well worth it to not feel scared, ashamed or confused about your bits.

So what actually is going on down there? Please excuse my terrible drawings, I'm not an artist.

The Vulva

Hannah Diagram 1

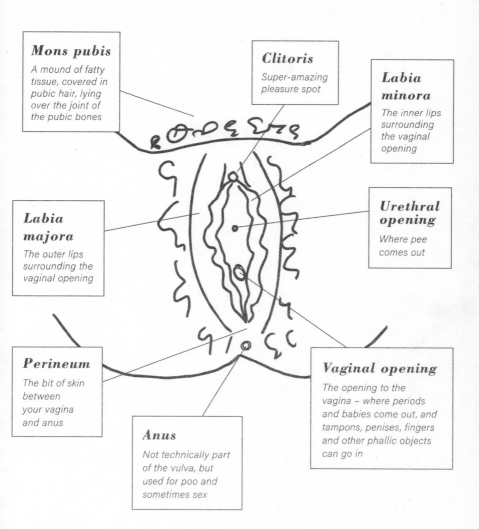

Mons pubis
A mound of fatty tissue, covered in pubic hair, lying over the joint of the pubic bones

Clitoris
Super-amazing pleasure spot

Labia minora
The inner lips surrounding the vaginal opening

Labia majora
The outer lips surrounding the vaginal opening

Urethral opening
Where pee comes out

Perineum
The bit of skin between your vagina and anus

Anus
Not technically part of the vulva, but used for poo and sometimes sex

Vaginal opening
The opening to the vagina – where periods and babies come out, and tampons, penises, fingers and other phallic objects can go in

This area is called the 'vulva'. The 'vagina' is the inside tunnel leading from the vaginal opening. So the vulva describes everything that is on the outside, whereas the vagina is internal.

A few words on body hair

Everywhere we look, the women in films, on TV and in adverts have smooth legs and are wearing bikinis without a single pubic hair poking out. Society places a certain expectation on women to shave, wax, pluck, thread, laser – basically to remove all hair. I just want to take a few moments to say you do want you want with your hair. If you love the feeling of soft hairs as you run your fingers over your legs (like Katniss Everdeen) then don't shave it off just because other people are. I feel like we're getting closer to accepting women doing what they want with their bodies, but there's still a long way to go. I have a lot of conflicting and confusing personal thoughts around body hair. In theory, I know and believe that I can do whatever I like with my body hair, and sometimes my legs get super hairy and I don't mind (but it's usually because I'm growing it out before getting a wax). Before I go on holiday I like to get a bikini wax to make sure no stray pubes ruin my sunbathing aesthetic. And there's a certain irony to writing about body hair when this morning I did a casual trim of the pubes. I still haven't figured out why I do this. Is it because I feel a certain pressure from society to be smooth if my legs/crotch are going to be out in public, or that I'm scared a sexual partner won't find me desirable if I'm hairy? I'm not going to lie, it's probably partly that because I do live in a society that is sending me those messages and I'm not bulletproof. But I also know that I like my smooth legs and my little hairy patch on my mons pubis. I weirdly like going to get them waxed. Or have I just trained myself to enjoy my own oppression? Am I experiencing Stockholm Syndrome with the patriarchy? Maybe don't think about it as much as I do, and just do whatever you feel comfortable with.

The Clitoris

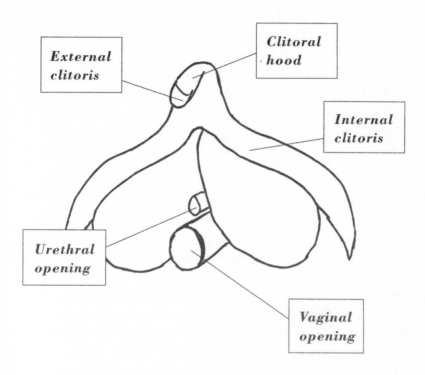

External clitoris

Clitoral hood

Internal clitoris

Urethral opening

Vaginal opening

I want to talk about the clitoris, OK? I just really love the clitoris. It is an incredible organ. I know I've mentioned this before but I want to reiterate it because it's so important: the clitoris is the only body part in all human bodies whose sole purpose is pleasure. That is the only reason it's there, for sexual pleasure. The clitoris contains 8,000 nerve endings – that's twice as many as a penis. It's found on bio-sex female bodies and I would speculate that the insane power and mystery of the clitoris is one of the reasons why, throughout history and still to this day, female sexuality is monitored, policed and punished. What would the world look like if women knew what their bodies were capable of? Heaven forbid. Something that I was definitely not taught in biology class, though, is that the clitoris you can see at the top of the vulva is just the tip of the iceberg. The whole clitoris extends inside the body, it wraps around the vagina and it's huge!

Pretty incredible, right? Who knew that was inside? Well, quite a lot of people actually – doctors, teachers, parents – but they all forgot to tell me about it for some reason.

As well as the clitoris, there are a lot of other things going on internally in a bio-sex female body. I have personally been very confused about one of these things for years. The cervix. You hear the word 'cervix' a lot when talking about anatomy and reproduction and I've always felt pretty comfortable with it. However, one day I realised that if someone asked me what the cervix is, where it was and what it did I wouldn't actually be able to give them an answer because I have no idea. When characters on TV shows were giving birth and the doctor talked about how dilated they were, for years I thought this was referring to the vaginal opening but no, they're talking about the cervix. Apparently, it's a narrow tunnel that connects the vagina and the uterus. Who knew?! Not me.

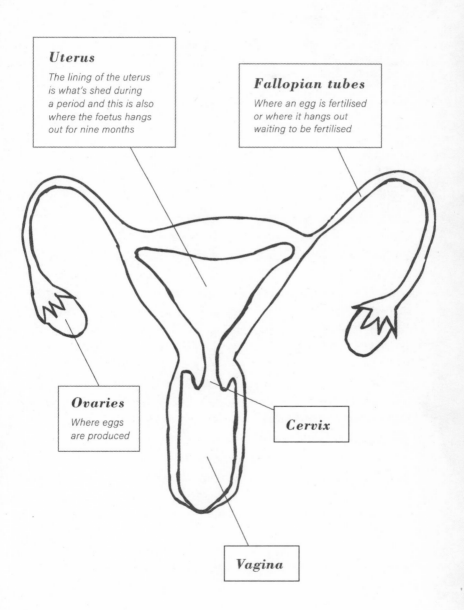

Uterus
The lining of the uterus is what's shed during a period and this is also where the foetus hangs out for nine months

Fallopian tubes
Where an egg is fertilised or where it hangs out waiting to be fertilised

Ovaries
Where eggs are produced

Cervix

Vagina

Periods

I was an early developer in everything other than height, and I wasn't even a late developer in that. I just remained short. I started secondary school at 11 years old, already wearing bras, and then a few months later, before I turned 12, I started my period. I actually really love the story of how I started my period, which is a sentence I don't know how many people can say. I was going to the cinema with my mum, my best friend and her mum, and we were going to see *Freaky Friday*. There's a definite mum-daughter vibe going on here. After the film was over, I went to the toilet and saw that there was some blood in my knickers. I knew exactly what was happening so I just grabbed a load of tissue paper, shoved it in my pants and when we got home I told my mum. She already had a stash of sanitary pads and tampons ready for when my sister and I started so there was no hassle at all. A bit of a non-event really. I remember wanting to feel this overwhelming sensation that I was now a woman and everything would be different, but there was no transformative spiritual occurrence, I'd just started bleeding.

For years my mum was the only person who knew that I'd started my period. Not sure how I managed to keep it secret but no one in school was talking about it. I didn't know if any of my friends had also started and I felt weirdly ashamed and embarrassed about the whole thing. So I didn't say anything. That was until I was about 13 and a bunch of us were hanging out at a friend's house and without warning she just got up, grabbed a tampon out of a drawer, waved it at us and then went to the toilet. I have never felt such relief – she had broken the ice and suddenly we were all talking about periods. One or two of my friends hadn't started theirs but others had, and we were telling stories of how we started, tips on dealing with PMS and just cracking jokes together about the whole thing. It felt so good to talk about it.

A few words on menstruation and blood

It is normal. It is not gross. It is just blood. It happens to half the world's population once a month for a good 30–40 years of their lives. Why are we so quiet about it? So hush-hush? And why do some of the other half, who just happen to have been born with different genitals and a different reproductive system, seem so disgusted by this? There are people who could go through their whole life without ever having seen a drop of period blood, whereas they will have seen gallons upon gallons of violent blood in films and on TV. On screen, we are numb to the kind of blood that we would hope never to have to see in real life, and it's completely normalised. Blood that comes from a vagina, however, we never see that. Photos get removed from Instagram, and in films periods are portrayed as disgusting or used as comedic devices to embarrass women and confuse men. I don't want to hear 'ew gross' from my friends if I mention that I'm on my period. I'm already dealing with the fact that my uterus is shredding its lining, I don't want to have to listen to you try and shame me and I don't have the time or energy to educate you. Periods happen. And no one should be made to feel ashamed about a natural bodily process. I'm not saying run around the streets waving around your used tampons (or only if you want to) I'm just saying that all of us have got a lot of unlearning to do in terms of how we talk and feel about periods.

OK, *what the hell is actually happening to my body?*

When you first start your period they can be quite irregular but in three to six months they should become regular, and you can track your period and your cycle. Other things can affect your period such as your weight, diet, exercise, general health and stress levels, so if you haven't had a period in a while or you're in your late teens and you haven't started yet it's a good idea to go and see your doctor. When I was seven years old I was diagnosed with ulcerative colitis, which is an inflammatory bowel disease, and I had flare-ups of symptoms when I was nine, 12, 14 and then 15 years old. I would be ill for several months before the medication helped me back into remission and during the times when I was ill I didn't have any periods. It was as if my body had gone, 'we can only deal with one thing at a time here, shut the periods down, shut it down.' Our bodies are so clever.

But because my body was in such turmoil, I never had regular periods, they were always late and I would bleed about every two months instead. To be honest, with everything else going on at school and all the things you have to deal with as a teenager, I'm kind of glad of this – a little silver lining to my Ulcerative Colitis. Although I never knew when I was going to come on, it was always a surprise so I had to be stocked up on pads and tampons at all times. I was also very lucky in that I never really experienced bad PMS. I occasionally got cramps but they were never so bad that I had to take painkillers and my mood was always fairly stable, my period never made me sad. But others aren't as lucky as me.

PMS or PMDD?

Everyone has heard of PMS (premenstrual syndrome), which usually affects people in the week before they have a period. It is the main term that gets thrown around to describe experiencing cramps, bloating, breast pains, mood swings, feeling irritable and all those other frustrating and painful symptoms. But PMS is manageable and shouldn't stop you from doing anything. With a healthy diet, exercise routine, relieving stress and regular sleep, it should be a breeze. However, according to the NHS around one in 20 people who have periods (so that's quite a lot) experience such severe symptoms that it can stop them from living their normal lives. This is because they have a more extreme version of PMS called PMDD (premenstrual dysphoric disorder). So if you feel completely debilitated when you're PMSing, or you feel like your PMS is interfering with work or social activities then it might be more serious.

You're not pathetic, weak or going 'crazy', PMDD is a real thing and you can go to your doctor to get advice on how to best manage and treat it.

Boobs
and bras

Breasts come in all shapes, sizes and colours, and the trick for them looking and feeling their best is to get a good bra. If you don't wear bras that's also totally fine, a lot of people with breasts don't for a variety of reasons, but if you do wear them it is so important you get fitted and you are wearing the correct-size bra. The best way to get a bra that fits perfectly is to be professionally measured, but here are some additional tips from me:

Throw away your tape measure 1

There are many different brands that make bras and they might have slight differences in their sizing.

2

Find the right back size

You want your bra strap to be horizontal across your back and not riding up. When trying on a bra, always fasten it on the loosest hook because with wear and wash the straps will stretch and so this leaves you adjustment room. If you pull the back strap away from your body there should be about a 1–2 inch gap.

3

Find the right cup size

The wires should lie flat against your breastbone in between your boobs. Make sure your boobs aren't bulging out the top or side, and that there is no spare material. You want to have a smooth line where the fabric of the cup meets your boobs.

4

Wear a t-shirt

When trying on bras for size, also check how they look in clothes.

And that's basically it! I am a 28FF and I don't know what I would do without properly fitted bras. Probably walk around in pain all day and never find clothes that look good.

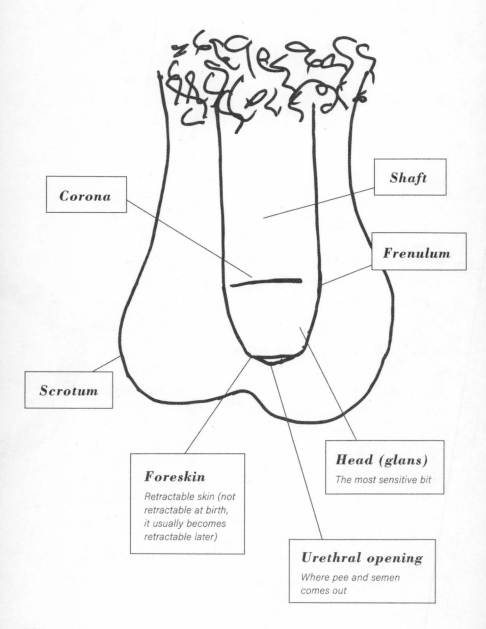

Corona

Shaft

Frenulum

Scrotum

Foreskin

Retractable skin (not retractable at birth, it usually becomes retractable later)

Head (glans)

The most sensitive bit

Urethral opening

Where pee and semen comes out

The Penis

In society in general, the penis is less of a mystery than the vulva, probably partly because everything is hanging out on full display. But there's still a lot going on.

The foreskin, kind of like the clitoral hood, covers the head, or glans, of the penis for protection. It's pretty flexible and you can pull it back to move up and down the glans of the penis.

Some penises are circumcised, which means that the foreskin has been removed. Circumcision is practised in certain countries and cultures when the child is still an infant. But some older children and adults may also have to be circumcised for medical reasons. Circumcision is a very controversial issue, with some cultures routinely circumcising babies and other people comparing it to FGM (Female Genital Mutilation). I'm Jewish (on my mother's side) and apparently the main thing that my parents argued about before I was born was whether or not I would be circumcised if I had a penis. But I came out with a vulva so they didn't have to worry about that.

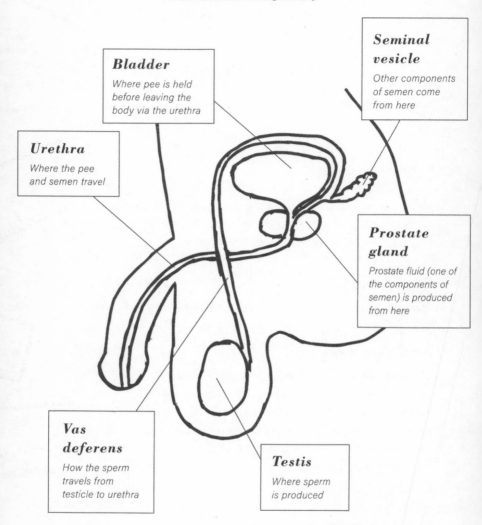

Seminal vesicle

Other components of semen come from here

Bladder

Where pee is held before leaving the body via the urethra

Urethra

Where the pee and semen travel

Prostate gland

Prostate fluid (one of the components of semen) is produced from here

Vas deferens

How the sperm travels from testicle to urethra

Testis

Where sperm is produced

About 70 per cent of semen comes from the seminal vesicle, and the rest comes from the prostate gland and the sperm in the testis. And all of that together makes semen, which is what comes out during ejaculation. The prostate is also a pleasure point on bio-sex men that can be stimulated through the anus.

A few words on penis size from
Calum McSwiggan

One of the most terrifying things about growing up as a boy is worrying about how you measure up in the trouser department. We're absolutely obsessed with having a big dick and we can be so wrought with the fear of being less than average that our days are filled with anxiety and panic. So many guys are terrified about anyone seeing them naked in case they don't measure up, but really all of this fear is baseless. Penis size really isn't as big a deal as people make it out to be and the idea that everyone has an 8-inch penis is completely untrue outside the world of porn. Many studies into penis size have concluded that the average erect penis is between 5 and 6 inches, and even if you do fall below that number it's nothing to worry about or obsess over. You may notice other boys in the locker room with much bigger penises but that's all down to the different rates we go through puberty. Our penises can carry on growing until our early twenties and by then you'll have completely forgotten why you were ever worried about it in the first place. Be proud of your penis because no matter how big or small it is, I can guarantee that someday it will make you, and somebody else, very happy indeed.

204

Body image and body confidence

In today's digital and very visual age, we receive a lot of messages about what the ideal body is, what is attractive and what is 'beautiful', in terms of size, shape, weight, height, skin colour, hair – in fact, anything you can think of that is part of our external appearance. And through these messages we are given a narrow list of 'acceptable' body types. We are told what is beautiful and made to assume that everything that doesn't fit these ideals is not beautiful. And sadly some people even see these 'other' bodies and appearances as 'ugly'. We do see some exceptions to this, but often the media's response is to say that they're 'so brave and cool', like it's a courageous act to just exist in this world and not look a certain way. Rather than just allowing different body types to be visible, they still have to be singled out and commented on. I would be lying if I said I was immune to this body standard I see everywhere. I sometimes wish my boobs were smaller, I'd like to be about six inches taller and I often hold in my stomach in front of the mirror or in photographs. But I recognise that somehow I've managed to dodge a bullet in terms of the extent to which it affects me. In general, I really do love my body. And I'm lucky, especially in this society, to be fairly slim and have somewhat of an hourglass figure. This is one of those 'check your privilege' moments and I certainly have thin-privilege. But some things cut much deeper than weight and the shape or size of your body doesn't make you immune to body issues. I could start talking about how it's important to love yourself and love your body, but let's be real, compliments from other people and external affirmation feel so good. There's nothing wrong with admitting that other people liking you makes you feel better about yourself, but it is important to have at least a foundation of self-love for that to build on. So here are some of my body confidence tips (you don't have to do all of them all at once). Feeling confident in your own skin can be a long journey, with ups and downs, so do what works for you and what you feel comfortable with. However, here's a list of some things you can try:

1 Take your clothes off

This might be something to build up to if you don't have a lot of body confidence to begin with, but it is so important. Being comfortable around yourself naked is such a great way to get to know your body and feel relaxed in your own skin. It may feel awkward at first but being naked in your own company is so rewarding.

2 Take a compliment

When people pay us compliments we have a tendency to ignore or deny them. Not taking compliments only re-affirms the negative feelings you may already have about yourself. Whereas if you take a compliment (even if you don't believe it at first) with a simple 'thank you', over time that can really help to build your confidence. When you give someone a compliment it feels so good when they accept it, so get into the habit of accepting other people's compliments.

3 Don't compare yourself to others

This is easier said than done but it is integral to feeling good about yourself. We all compare ourselves to others from time to time but doing it all the time is a toxic pattern to get into. Remember, even the people you're comparing yourself to probably have their own issues with body image and confidence. Comparisons don't help anyone: ultimately focusing on yourself will make you so much happier, too.

4 Focus on the things you like

Think of one physical thing you like about yourself. Every morning look at it in the mirror and say you like it. It can be your hair, your nose, your feet, your elbows – anything. When you pay attention to something that you like about yourself you're more likely to find more things that you like because you're thinking positively.

5 Change the things you can

A new haircut, clothes or a piercing can make us feel so good about ourselves. It's important to build a foundation of body confidence so that you're not always relying on these quick fixes but changing something about your appearance can still make you feel great.

6 Fake it 'til you make it

This doesn't work for everyone but it has certainly worked for me. Who we are doesn't just come from within ourselves, it also comes from how others perceive and treat us. If someone thinks you're SpongeBob SquarePants and starts treating you like you're SpongeBob SquarePants, over time you might actually start to think that you're SpongeBob SquarePants! OK, that's a weird example. But what I mean is, pretend to be confident even if you don't feel it. Other people will then think you're a confident person and treat you as such. Being treated a certain way can make you be that way, so fake it until you become it.

7 Exercise/do a sport

This isn't about losing weight or toning your body, no no no. People who exercise or do sport regularly generally feel much better and happier about themselves. It's all those happy hormones you release when you exercise!

8 Put action before appearance

Think of your body as a tool, rather than what it looks like. What are all the amazing things that it allows you to do? Eat, drink, walk, dance, play the piano, watch Netflix ... (you've got to be comfy and use your eyes – very important).

9 Check yourself

We all occasionally think negative things about ourselves or other people. You need to acknowledge when you've had a negative thought and stop it. Get into the habit of checking yourself when you criticise your own body or someone else's. It might be hard at first if you have these thoughts quite often, but if you get into the habit, it will become easier over time.

10 Wear what you want

We're constantly told that if you're a certain shape then you should or shouldn't wear certain styles of clothes, but I call BS on this. I used to think that because I have a short body and big boobs I couldn't wear crop tops. Well guess what, I really want to wear crop tops so I'm going to wear crop tops. Clothes should be made to fit us, we don't have to change to fit clothes. Wear the clothes that make you feel comfortable, confident and that you like.

11 Take what you see in the media with a pinch of salt

You're going to need more than a pinch. The images and celebrities you see mostly have a whole team styling them and then on top of that there's Photoshop. If you can, avoid these kinds of magazines completely, but if not try to understand that these 'ideals' you see aren't ideals at all and aren't even realistic for most people.

12 Social media lies

Even online, when the photos are coming directly from a person, on Instagram for example, everyone uses filters, and photos are always carefully selected to show people what you want them to see.

13 Distract yourself

Hang out with your friends, take up a hobby, focus on work or school. When you're fully in the moment it's very difficult to think of anything else. A great way to practise living in the moment is through mindfulness, so when you're out having fun you're not even thinking about what you look like.

14 Surround yourself with positive, supporting friends

Avoid people who say negative things about your body. Friends can offer all kinds of help and support when you're feeling down about yourself, so it's good to have positive people there for you. You will always be your own worst critic and sometimes it takes looking through someone else's eyes to see how beautiful you are.

A few words on muscles from
Calum McSwiggan

From a very early age boys have it drilled into them that their personal worth is associated with their masculinity and their muscle mass. Men with rippling biceps and washboard abs appear everywhere in the media and are seen as the pinnacle of desirability, and that in itself can leave a lot of us feeling deflated. It's important to remember that all of our bodies are different and all of us develop in different ways, particularly when we're going through puberty. Some of us will grow much broader and some of us will barely change at all – whatever the outcome for you, you shouldn't punish yourself for it. You may not be as thin or as tall or as muscly as the people around you but that's because your body is going through its own individual metamorphosis and that's what makes you unique. There will always be someone bigger or stronger than you but that doesn't make you any less attractive, desirable, or worthy. It's easy to get jealous of those who look different to ourselves, but it's always worth reminding yourself that they may be looking back at you and your body with a jealousy of their own.

Calum McSwiggan (@CalumMcSwiggan) is an LGBTQ+ writer and YouTuber who creates video content that covers everything from LGBTQ+ issues to dating, mental health, and sex education.

Michelle Elman on *Body image and Confidence*

I was 10 years old when it occurred to me that my body was different. It always had been, but age 10 was the first time I actually noticed it. The differences I am talking about are my scars – from 15 surgeries, a brain tumour, a punctured intestine, an obstructed bowel, a cyst in my brain and a condition called hydrocephalus. These scars made my body 'imperfect', and my dreams of attaining conventional beauty standards forever unobtainable. They were the source of my body woes and the bulk of my insecurities. At that age, I had only earned seven of my eventual 20+ surgery badges of honour and what adorned my abdomen was a bunch of lines that looked like an incomplete game of noughts and crosses. Over the next five years, I would add to this collection, eventually forming marks that largely resemble a smiley face, or, on a particularly fat day, a winky one. I wish I could say that the reason I was motivated to start loving my scars was for my own happiness, but it wasn't. It was for a boy, or more accurately, it was for the hope of a potential boy, because don't you know that 'confidence is the most attractive outfit'? Well

*that was one outfit not in my closet, probably
because it didn't come in my size. I was 15
when it occurred to me that my scars could
cause a problem in intimate relationships. I
was a virgin and hadn't even kissed a boy, yet
I was already worried about the inevitable
day that I would remove my top in front of
someone and there, instead of a washboard
set of abs, would be my lines winking back
at him. Much like when someone is watching
you try to pee, would my two faces suddenly
induce performance anxiety?*

*Whether you have scars or not, we've all had
that paranoia – the one where you strip down
naked and that special other person looks at
you with horror, or even disgust? Everyone
has had that thought at least once in their
life, because your body has no correlation to
your body confidence. Skinny people can be
insecure, fat people can be confident, male or
female, every human being in the world has
insecurities, so it makes sense that when you
are naked, at your most vulnerable, these
worries show themselves in the strongest way.
I wish my body confidence came before my
first intimate relationship but that wasn't
the case, and is rarely how it happens. More
likely than not, you will have awkward
moments, there will be that time you insist on*

keeping the lights off and occasionally you might selectively keep some of your clothing on in order to reveal as little of your body as possible. But all these experiences will help you create comfort in this new scenario.

It is a learning curve, so stop putting so much pressure on yourself to feel comfortable instantly. Personally, a large part of my confidence came from the realisation that people like sex. When a naked person is standing in front of another naked person, the last thing that person will do is turn down an opportunity to get laid, so you might as well eradicate that nightmare about someone walking out on you after you've gotten naked. Most probably, mainly what they will be thinking about when they see your naked body is sex. That might not be the most romantic notion but it does mean that they won't be analysing your body for flaws or imperfections. If anything, they will be thinking of their own insecurities and about how flattering the light is on their body.

Body confidence in the bedroom comes in waves. I used to feel that my personality could compensate for my body – that if I was an awesome-enough person, people would ignore my body flaws. I decided that my

love life could only be a possibility if I could figure out a way to get someone to love me in spite of my body. Then I discovered the real crux to body confidence: self-love. Berating and belittling my body and treating it like unwanted baggage was not the way to feel comfortable in my skin. Loving me means loving my body. Body confidence was about accepting all aspects of myself and that meant being kind to my body, scars and all.

My scars are part of my story. It is who I am and wearing these marks with pride is important to me – dismissing my scars is dismissing my past. A past which I am hugely proud to have survived. Now, I not only celebrate my body for what it looks like, but what it can do. And this works in the bedroom too: place more emphasis on action than appearances. Think of it as positive reinforcement, if you think of your body less in that situation, you get rewarded with an orgasm. Let's be honest, you can't fully let go and enjoy yourself if you are worrying about your stomach hanging out.

Michelle Elman (@mindset_forlife) is a body confidence coach and the founder of Mindset For Life, a company that works to build the confidence of women worldwide.

215

Jimmy Hill on *Body image*

It's a familiar scene: post-shower, standing naked in front of the mirror; ashamed by and angry at the reflection. No amount of poking, stretching, smoothing or hiding is improving the situation. There are no abs. There has been no discernible change in penis size, despite committed, regular exercise. There are no sticky-out shoulder bone things (clavicles? Or is that a musical instrument?). There is a developing man boob situation and there are still no pubes. This is isn't what I want to look like. I hate this and everyone else will too. Being a boy who hates their body is a complicated thing: a shitty mix of low confidence, rejection, puberty, dysphoria, sex, acne, genetics, genitals, bravado and biceps; all distilled by that most frustrating human pursuit – comparing yourself to others.

It took me a long time to 'accept' my body, and for many years (14–18) I was paralysed by a persistent and severe loathing of what I looked like. Of course, I never talked about it – why would I? I'm male. We don't talk about stuff. We play football and invent stories about fingering girls behind bushes. I never did anything about it either, because, well, what can you do? You can't make your voice break faster, you can't grow taller overnight, and, despite the wild claims of certain dubious websites, you absolutely can't enlarge your dick using just some string and a kitchen spoon … Not that I've tried. Obviously. You're kind of just stuck with what you've got, and weirdly, looking back, what I had was actually pretty normal. I was a bit of a 'late developer' in that puberty took its sweet time, and I was a little bit chubby (hi Monster Munch), but other than that, you certainly wouldn't have picked me out of a group of lads as the hideous, Voldermort-like freak I imagined I was. So why the low self-esteem? Why the embarrassment? Why the horrible sadness?

I think to really understand it, you have to think about what it is to be a boy. It's not really about appearances – it's about struggling to fit in and psychologically make sense of what being male is. Boys are bombarded with a confusing mess of standards (most of them bad for the world) and a perplexing moral code. I should be strong, brave, good at sport, attractive to women, respected by men, masculine, dominating, handsome, straight ...

If you're one of the majority who don't possess all of these characteristics, you're probably going to feel short-changed and end up somewhere on the 'I don't like my body' scale, or worse: 'I don't like myself'. The majority of male body image issues come from feeling like you're not 'man enough' – a meaningless aspiration made worse by the fact that everyone hits puberty at a different time. Everyone gets those signifiers of 'masculinity' at varying ages – two 14-year-old boys can look vastly different, simply because they've hit puberty at different times. Beyond frustrating, when all anyone wants is to 'fit in'. Boys don't talk about their bodies or worries, meaning I internalised my fears and insecurities and continued to compare myself to the more 'developed' boys in my class with abs, facial hair and seemingly endless self-confidence. Sneaky glances in the changing room led to crushing paranoia and shame. I kept my head down at school; I became shy and withdrawn. I thought about it all the time. I felt like an outcast.

The sad thing is, my experience is so common, I'm sure it is, but we don't know exactly how widespread it is because men are all too f*cking scared of losing face to talk about it. Jokes about dick size and man boobs are seen as harmless, in the same way that fetishising Tom Daley's rippling abs is viewed as perfectly acceptable, but these messages damage young boys. Gender and body ideals are no good for anyone, regardless of sex, and it's important to think about the whole picture. We need to talk about it more.

I worry about boys. I worry that they feel excluded from conversations about body image and don't recognise the pressure they're putting on themselves. I hope that as discussions about appearance and expectation become more common things will get easier, but we need to make sure boys are included. For people struggling with this now, here's my advice:

Realise that the 'perfect body' is made up. It doesn't exist. It's a concept that's been around in various forms since the genesis of civilisation, but it's always been based on the human imagination. A body is just a body. Your physical appearance does not correlate to your worth as a human. Don't dwell on your appearance. The more you obsess over what you look like, the more of an issue it will become. Enjoy your body. Look for things to love. Bodies are amazing and interesting and fun. Appreciate that. Know that over time you will grow into your body, physically and mentally. Once you're through puberty, things get so much easier. Trust me. Don't let your body hold you back. No one is a better person because they have what society deems a 'good' body. For the most part, you can't really change your appearance, but you can be the person you want to be – focus on the positive changes you can make and rise above superficial nonsense. Concentrate on being a self-confident, happy, fulfilled person. Surround yourself with people who care about who you are, not what you look like.

Most importantly, when you find yourself back at that mirror, checking out your naked body, remember that you are capable of loving how you look, but it doesn't take a change in appearance: it takes a change in mindset. A change that I guarantee will improve your happiness immeasurably.

Jimmy Hill (@hi_jimmy) is a TV presenter and vlogger, who makes videos on life, relationships and sexuality.

Chapter 9

sexual pleasure

*I*n school we're taught about the reproductive system – all the internal stuff like the uterus and fallopian tubes and testicles and sperm and eggs, because that's how we make babies and that's science. But anything to do with pleasure is conveniently left out. A friend of mine who used to teach sex and relationships education in schools said that she would ask the kids to write down any questions they had anonymously on a piece of paper and then at the end she would answer them. I asked her the most common question, and to my surprise it was,

'*If Mum and Dad don't want any more babies, why do they still have sex?*'

I hadn't even thought about this before but one of the (many) things we leave out of sex education is that sex feels good. If you're lucky to get any kind of sex education from your school or from your parents then I bet it was mostly about how to avoid it for as long as possible, how to *not* get pregnant, how to *not* get an STI and how to *not* get raped. Which is ridiculous. Yes, we should be giving young people basic tools such as knowing when they want to have sex and when they don't, and information about contraception and STIs. But whilst they're important, if they are the only conversations you have around the topic of sex then it paints a pretty negative picture of it. As something to fear: something that could lead to unwanted things happening to your body. We forget to include all the amazing stuff. The fact that sex is pleasurable shouldn't be kept a secret. And you can understand that something has the potential to feel good without actually doing it. You can be aware of the benefits of sex whilst knowing that you're not ready personally.

So it is my mission to bring sexual pleasure on to the sex and relationships education curriculum. Pleasure is important! Why do we have sex if we don't want to have a baby? There are loads of reasons that people have sex – some good, some bad – but needless to say it's a lot more complex than 'I want a baby'. Here are just a few:

Feeling close and connected to someone else

Satisfying sexual desires

As an expression of love and feeling loved

Out of boredom

Curiosity

You're attracted to the person

Because of insecurities

To boost self-esteem

To have an orgasm

Affection

To improve mood

It's fun

You feel horny

To please your partner

Excitement / adventure

It feels good

Stress relief

Sex feels good. And there's nothing wrong or shameful about admitting that. Hey, I like sex. I love sex. Wow, it feels so good to just say that. **I LOVE SEX.**

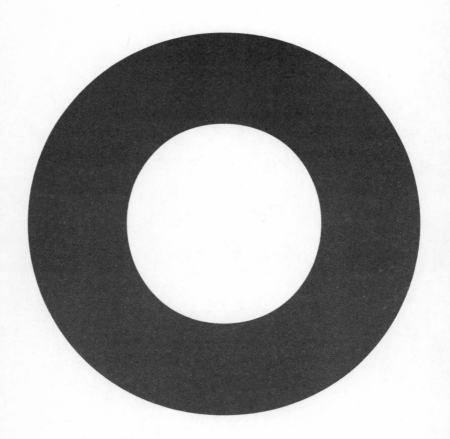

Orgasm

The main thing that people use to quantify sexual pleasure is the orgasm. The big O. So first of all, what is going on in your body when you build up to and have an orgasm?

Excitement

Plateau

Orgasm

Resolution

When you're getting aroused, this stage is called 'excitement'. It builds and it builds, maybe taking some dips along the way. Remember sex doesn't have to be a linear experience. Your excitement stage doesn't have to be a straight line going up, it can be more of a wave. This is the point where you're trying different things, different kisses, strokes, touches, pressures, speeds, etc. The plateau is what I like to call 'the point of no return'. You can feel that an orgasm is imminent and when you're plateauing the best way to reach orgasm is repetition, repetition, repetition. Just whatever it is you're doing, keep doing it. Then the orgasm is that incredible, explosive feeling, like a sense of relief. And resolution is probably better described as 'recovery'. Some orgasms really do feel like you have to recover from them.

But human beings are complex and so are orgasms. Sometimes you might build and build and never get there, and that's fine.

Sometimes you might plateau, have an orgasm, then another and (maybe another) and then resolution. Other times you might plateau and then stop, build again and stop, and repeat for as long as you can bear (this is called edging) and then when you finally have an orgasm it feels incredible. Worth the wait. So there are a lot of variations of types of orgasm you can have. Some of them may take time and practice to perfect, so maybe go on a bit of an orgasm adventure (by yourself or with a partner). It's always fun exploring what your body can do. It's also important to remember that orgasm doesn't necessarily mean ejaculation. Even for people with penises, you can have an orgasm without ejaculating. They often happen at the same time, but they are different. If you have a penis, you usually have to wait a while after ejaculating before you can go again, but you can still have more than one orgasm before you ejaculate. Again, practice! Whatever kind of orgasms you have, how often, on your own or with a partner, under certain circumstances but not others – you are normal. Everyone's bodies are different and orgasms can be complicated. They can be affected by other factors, too, like stress and alcohol. If you're unhappy with your orgasms then you can always talk to someone about it: friends (someone might have experienced a similar thing and be able to help); your partner (maybe you can work together); an expert – remember there is no shame in seeking help from a doctor, counsellor, therapist or clinical sexologist if there's something in your sex life that you're unsatisfied with. If sex is important to you then find a way to make it fulfilling.

Faking it

We all know the famous scene from *When Harry Met Sally*. If you don't, put down this book, search for the 'fake orgasm scene in *When Harry Met Sally*' on Youtube, watch it, and then come back. OK, now we're all educated in my favourite rom-com of all time, we can talk about the idea of faking it. First of all, people with penises can fake orgasms too. (Remember the whole orgasm-not-equalling-ejaculation thing?) But, it is more of a trend, shall we say, among people with vaginas.

I have never faked an orgasm. When I tell people that, they are shocked – most people say that they've definitely faked it at least once. Before I had my first orgasm I was still having sex, but just orgasm-less sex. It doesn't mean I didn't enjoy it! But I never faked it. I don't know why I was so comfortable telling my sexual partners that I'd never have an orgasm but I'm glad I was. Also, because I'd never had one I had no idea how to fake it so it would look real. All I had to go on was *When Harry Met Sally*!

Many people do fake it, though, and for all sorts of reasons. Because it's easier, you don't want to insult the other person, you're tired and want it to be over, you're too scared to ask for what you really want, you faked it that other time ... If you fake it one time then you're more likely to feel like you have to fake it again. And then your partner thinks they're doing a great job and know exactly how to get you off. The longer you leave it, the more awkward it'll be when you have to tell them that actually you need something a little bit different. You can avoid all that awkwardness by just communicating clearly in the first place what turns you on and what works for you.

Again, though, easier said than done, especially if you're already far down the 'faking it' road, or lacking the time or energy to teach the other person exactly what you like. But either way, it's important to feel comfortable to ask for what you want and be honest if you don't have an orgasm. Sex isn't this goal-orientated thing where an orgasm is the ultimate achievement. It's the whole process, the 'session', and having an orgasm is not the be-all and end-all. If you know you can have an orgasm with a partner then it'll be totally worth your time to teach them how, and if you know it's not going to happen this time then there is no shame in that. You can say at any point that you're done and want to stop.

I want everyone to feel super-comfortable in themselves, their sex lives, and giving and receiving pleasure, and one way to achieve that is to stop faking and start communicating.

What is 'real' sex like?

Part of sexual pleasure is knowing the reality of it, the fun of it, sometimes the silliness of it. Sex in films gave me very unrealistic expectations. I thought it would be slow, romantic, clothes coming off sensually, silk sheets, grabbing hold of headboards, cuddles and kisses afterwards. But no. Here are some things I feel I need to share about the reality of sex. Some of them can be awkward and maybe not 'sexy' but if you just embrace the humour, they can still make sex really fun and pleasurable:

All the juices and liquids

– sweat, lube, semen, vaginal juices, period blood (sometimes). There's a lot going on, things can get messy

Farting & queefing (fanny fart)

– it happens to the best of us

Squeaky beds

– a great way to resolve this is to put the pillows and duvet on the floor and have sex on the floor. You're welcome!

Awkward positions

that don't work, or taking a while to get into a comfortable position

Accidental elbows & knees

flying all over the place and bashing into each other

Breasts

getting in the way or clapping together (I like to think they're giving me a constant applause)

Hair getting in the way

– if you have long hair always have a hair tie nearby (very useful!)

PEE AFTER SEX

– yes I know you want to just lie there and kiss and cuddle and sleep but there's a more urgent thing to do here. If you have a vagina, when you're done, get up and go to the toilet. I wish someone had told me this earlier in life, it would have saved me from several UTIs (urinary tract infections).

So sex doesn't have to be sexy but all these things don't have to take away from the experience. They can be funny, and you know you've found a good sexual partner when you can laugh about these things together.

So embrace the weird and wonderful and pleasurable world of sex!

Chapter 10

contraception

IT JUST TAKES
ONE PERSON TO
SAY SOMETHING
OUT LOUD AND
THEN WE CAN
START TO HELP
AND SUPPORT
EACH OTHER
BY SHARING
OUR OWN
EXPERIENCES.

If you are having the type of sex that could lead to pregnancy, you also need to think about contraception.

Contraception refers to the methods used to prevent unwanted pregnancies if you still want to have and enjoy sex. Sex is risky. There really isn't any such thing as 'safe' sex – the only way to be 100 per cent safe is to not have sex at all, but that's unrealistic for a lot of people. However, there are many ways to have safer sex. First of all, condoms are the only contraception that will protect you from unwanted pregnancy *and* STIs. All the other forms of contraception only work in preventing unwanted pregnancies, so always use a condom. Contraception is something that most sexually active teenagers and adults use but it's rarely discussed that openly. My main piece of advice before you decide what contraception to use is to talk to people about it. If you're in a relationship talk to your partner about what you think would work best for you. Do you know what contraception most of your friends use? Find out! Sometimes to me it feels like we're all silently struggling with the same thing – it just takes one person to say something out loud and then we can start to help and support each other by sharing our own experiences. Bodies are complex and your doctor can list all the common side effects of certain methods but sometimes it can help more to hear one of your friends talk about how being on the pill gave them lighter periods, or made them put on weight, or balanced out their mood, or gave them really bad period pains. So talk about it. But also don't expect your body to react in the same way. Everyone is different. That's one of the annoying things about contraception. You never know how it's going to affect you until you try it, and then it can become a game of trial and error until you find the perfect fit. Or maybe you'll never find the perfect one for you and you'll always have to deal with some side effects. What a joy. Can someone please invent a test already that we can do to measure our hormones and physiology or something and then put us on the best contraception from the beginning? That'd be great, thanks.

Different types of contraception

Which method you choose is entirely up to you, how your body works and your lifestyle. There are some that you have to take every day, or every time you have sex, or there are some that last months or years. There are a lot of options to choose from and hopefully you'll find one that suits you. Most of these methods are available for free from your GP or local sexual health or family planning clinic.

(These are all preventative methods, we'll look at emergency methods later.)

Method	How it works
Male (external) condoms	Covers the penis to stop semen coming into contact with the vagina.
Female (internal) condoms	Goes inside the vagina to stop semen coming into contact with the vagina.
Combined pill	Contains oestrogen and progestogen. It stops eggs being released from the ovaries, it makes it harder for the sperm to reach the egg, it makes the uterus lining thinner so a fertilised egg cannot implant.
Progestogen -only pill	It thickens the lining of your cervix, making it difficult for sperm to pass through and reach an egg. It sometimes stops your ovaries from releasing an egg (if it also contains desogestrel).

How often?

Pros/Cons

Every time you have sex.

They are easy and effective. Some people complain about them 'ruining the moment' or 'not feeling as good', but don't let this stop you from using them!

98% effective

Every time you have sex – you can put it in up to eight hours before.

Can put it in hours before sex so it doesn't 'ruin the moment', but is less commonly used than the male condom.

95% effective

Every day at the same time for 21 days and then take a week break. (Unless you have the one with placebo pills – then you take it for the full 28 days). This week break, or when you take the placebo pills, is when you have a 'withdrawal bleed'.

Doesn't interrupt sex, no long-term effects to fertility, can help with heavy/painful periods, PMS and acne, but you have to remember to take it every day and it can have some side effects such as headaches, nausea, tender breasts, mood swings and blood spotting when you first start.

Over 99% effective

Every day for 28 days and repeat. Some pills you have to take within a three-hour window, others within 12 hours.

The same as the combined pill except it's good for people who can't have oestrogen. It may cause irregular periods – they may happen less often or stop completely.

Over 99% effective

Diaphragms and caps

You insert it to cover the cervix to stop semen from entering the vagina. It's recommended that you also use spermicide (a gel that kills sperm). It must be fitted by a doctor or nurse the first time.

Implant

Long Acting Reversible Contraception (LARC). A 4cm-long stick (the size of a matchstick) is inserted under the skin in your arm by a doctor or nurse. Contains progestogen. Stops ovulation, thickens mucus around the cervix and thins the uterus lining.

Injection

LARC method containing progestogen. It's injected into muscle, usually in your bum or upper arm. It stops ovulations, thickens the mucus around the cervix and thins the uterus lining.

IUD
'The copper coil'

Small T-shaped plastic device containing copper. It's inserted into the womb through the vagina by a doctor. It contains no hormones. Copper is toxic to sperm so it works by preventing sperm from surviving in the cervix, uterus and fallopian tubes.

IUS

Small T-shaped plastic device that contains progestogen. The hormones are localised in the womb only. It's inserted into the womb through the vagina by a doctor. Thickens the mucus in the cervix, thins the uterus lining and stops ovulation in some women.

Every time you have sex. Put it in before you have sex and you have to leave it in for at least six hours afterwards.	Does not disturb your menstrual cycle or interrupt sex (although add extra spermicide if you have sex more than three hours after putting it in) but it can take a while to get used to and you can't use it on your period.	**92-96% effective with spermicide**
It lasts tree years after it's inserted or until you get it taken out (if sooner).	Doesn't interrupt sex and once you have it put in you don't have to think about it. It's an option for those who can't have oestrogen. But you may have similar side effects to the pill and your period may be irregular or stop completely.	**Over 99% effective**
Depending on which type you get it can last up to eight, 12 or 13 weeks.	Similar to the implant except the injection lasts the full length of time because you cannot get it removed. Side effects may include bone thinning but this usually recovers once the injections stop.	**Over 99% effective**
Lasts five to 10 years depending on the type.	Can be used by those who can't or don't wish to take hormonal contraception, but periods may be heavier, more painful or last longer. There's a small risk of the IUD being pushed out or displaced, and it can cause pain and discomfort when it's inserted.	**Over 99% effective**
Lasts three to five years depending on the type.	It can help with painful or heavy periods and is an option for those who can't use oestrogen. Can make periods lighter, shorter or stop completely. Similar side effects to other hormonal contraception and has the same cons as the IUD.	**Over 99% effective**

Patch	It's a small patch that you put on the skin like a plaster. It contains oestrogen and progestogen. It stops ovulation and thins the lining of the uterus.
Vaginal ring	A soft plastic ring that goes inside the vagina. It releases oestrogen and progestogen. It stops ovulation, thickens the mucus in the cervix and thins the lining of the uterus.
Female sterilisation	The fallopian tubes are cut, sealed or blocked so that no sperm can reach the egg. Periods will continue.
Male sterilisation	The tube that carries sperm from the testicles to the penis is cut and sealed or tied.
Fertility awareness or natural family planning	This works by figuring out when you are fertile during your cycle and avoiding unprotected sex during this time. Must be taught by a specialist. You monitor your body temperature, cervical mucus, and the length of your menstrual cycle.

You wear the patch for one week, then change it every week for three weeks. You then have a patch-free week where you have a withdrawal bleed.

It doesn't interrupt sex and you don't have to remember it every day. It can make your periods lighter and more regular and it can help to reduce PMS and improve acne. Similar side effects to other hormonal contraception. The patch may cause skin irritation, and it is visible, unlike other contraception.

Over 99% effective

You wear one ring for 21 days and then take it out (and throw it away) and have a seven-day break where you'll have a withdrawal bleed before replacing it. You can insert and remove it yourself at home.

It is easy to insert yourself and you only have to think about it every 21 days. It can make your periods lighter, more regular and reduce pains. May have similar side effects to other hormonal contraception and may cause vaginal irritation and discharge.

Over 99% effective

Permanent method for those who don't want children or don't want any more children. It takes between four weeks and three months for it to be effective.

Don't have to think about contraception but it is very difficult to reverse. It's uncommon but tubes can re-join.

Over 99% effective

As with female sterilisation.

As with female sterilisation.

Over 99% effective

It involves monitoring and recording your natural body signs such as your temperature every day of your cycle to determine your fertile days.

It can be used to avoid and plan pregnancy and doesn't involve taking hormones or using physical devices, but it takes commitment and involves keeping daily records. It takes a few months to figure out your exact cycle and fertile days. If you get ill it can make results hard to interpret and can be difficult if you have an irregular cycle.

Over 99% effective (around 75% with mistakes)

How to put a condom on

When I was 14 years old, the school nurse came to our PSHE (Personal, Social Health Education) class to teach us about contraception. In groups we were given a test tube and a condom – although now that I think about it, what we were preparing to put condoms on are a bit wider than the test tubes we were practising on ... Everyone in my group was squeamish and didn't want to touch the condom (and people are worried about young people being too sexualised – we didn't even want to touch a gross slimy condom). Anyway, sex education was clearly in my blood because I stepped up and said I'd do it. I took the condom out of the wrapper and rolled it over the test tube. But then, it started to roll back up. The nurse came over to take a look and told me that I'd put it on the wrong way around ... whoops! Good job I practised on a test tube before putting one on a penis, eh? So here's how to do it properly:

1 | *Check the expiration date. Expired condoms are more likely to break. **There's an expiration date for a reason.***

2 | *Rip the wrapper along the edge and **DO NOT use your teeth.** You don't want to ruin the condom before you've even used it, and it doesn't matter how sexy you look opening a condom wrapper with your teeth – **no one wants a punctured condom.***

3 *Make sure it's the right way around – **it should look like a little hat and roll outwards.** Test it to make sure it's rolling the right way.*

4 *Pinch the top of the condom and place it on top of the penis. This keeps air out – **trapped air can cause a condom to break.***

5 *Roll it down the shaft of the penis. If it's inside out throw the condom away and use a different one. **Do not turn it the other way around and put it back on**. There may already be pre-cum on it.*

6 *__Lube it up if you fancy.__ But make sure you use a water-based lube (not oil-based). If you don't believe me, try blowing up a condom and rubbing Vaseline on it.*

7 *Have fun!*

8 *When you withdraw, **hold the condom at the base** – this prevents it from slipping off.*

9 *Take off the condom, **tie it in a knot** and throw it in the bin.*

Congratulations, you've successfully used a condom! You can buy condoms in most pharmacies and in toilets in some bars and clubs, but you can also get them for free from the doctor or sexual health clinics. (Another use for condoms is blowing them up into balloons and drawing faces on them. It would be a lie to say I haven't done this.)

Emergency contraception and abortion

So what happens if you don't use contraception for whatever reason, or your chosen method has failed you? Well, if you don't want to get pregnant and have a child then there are still options. There's the emergency contraceptive pill, the IUD and abortion. But remember, these methods should never be used as contraception, they are for emergencies only (except the IUD). It's not healthy to take the emergency contraceptive pill every time you have unprotected sex, and no one plans on having an abortion.

Emergency contraception

I've had to take the emergency contraceptive pill twice in my life so far. I'm not planning on having to take it again but you never know what life is going to throw at you ... The first time was when I was 16 and then again when I was 17. Both times it was because the condom broke and I wasn't on the pill. Definite mood killer. So I went off to the pharmacy and my partner came with me for moral support. In the UK you can just buy the emergency contraceptive pill over the counter but it's quite expensive and we couldn't afford it, so I had to answer a few questions from the specialist before they gave it to me for free. Other than the horrible feeling of anxiety and worry, the whole process went very smoothly and I was very relieved when I got my next period. I was given a lot of warnings about the emergency contraceptive pill because it pumps your body with a lot of hormones to stop you from getting pregnant. My mum has taken it before too and she said it made her feel really sick, but I didn't feel anything. Lucky me! My mum reckons it might be a sign that I'll have a very easy pregnancy in the future, but let's not think about that just now.

So if you've had unprotected sex or you think contraception has failed you and you want to prevent a pregnancy then you have two options: the emergency contraceptive or the 'morning after' pill, or the IUD.

The emergency contraceptive pill (EC):

Even though it is called the 'morning after' pill, you don't have to wait until the next morning to take it. The sooner you take it after you've had unprotected sex, the more effective it is. Depending on which pill you take, it can either be taken up to 72 hours (three days) or 120 hours (five days) after you've had unprotected sex, but the effectiveness decreases the longer you leave it. EC works by preventing or delaying ovulation, and it can make your period come earlier or later than usual. EC can make you feel sick, dizzy, or tired and can cause headaches, tender breasts and abdominal pain. If you vomit within two hours of taking it, you may have vomited it out so go to an expert because you may need to take it again. One thing to remember is that the EC is not an abortion and it doesn't cause abortion, it prevents conception. When I was at school there were a lot of urban myths around the morning after pill, for example that it's so strong you can only take it up to three times in your whole lifetime. At 17, having already taken two, I thought I was doing horrible things to my body and running out of lives, like a video game. But I was worrying for nothing because that's not the case. There's no limit to how many you can take in your lifetime but it is still for emergencies only. Make sure you are using a different form of contraception if you don't want to get pregnant.

IUD:

The 'copper coil', as well as being a long-term method of contraception, can also be used in an emergency. It works by stopping an egg implanting in your uterus, and has to be fitted by a doctor or nurse within five days of unprotected sex. If you have the IUD fitted as an emergency contraceptive then you can continue to use it as normal contraception.

Abortion

So that's how you prevent a pregnancy, but what if you find out you're pregnant and for whatever reason don't want to have the baby? A third of women in the UK will have an abortion by the time they're 45. That number shocked me when I first heard it – but it probably seems high because it isn't really something people talk about that much. In Britain abortion is legal up to 24 weeks if two doctors agree that continuing the pregnancy will cause you physical or mental distress, and it is free on the NHS. The first thing to remember is that the decision is completely up to you. It's your body, it's your pregnancy and the choice is yours. However, it's always a good idea to talk it out as well, with your partner, family and friends. It can be a tough decision to make and you might want to have support from the people around you. That said, you don't have to tell anyone if you don't want to, and your doctor won't either. There are different kinds of abortions depending on how far along you are in your pregnancy. Abortions are very safe but, like every medical procedure, they come with some risks. If you are pregnant and considering having an abortion, check out the resources in the back of this book, seek out the support you need and remember what you do is your choice and no one else's.

The
Hormone Diaries

When I was 17 I decided to go on the Pill. I was in a long-term relationship and my boyfriend and I wanted to stop using condoms (we'd both been tested for STIs). Because of some other medication I was on, I couldn't use contraception with oestrogen in it and so I started taking Cerazette, which is a progestogen-only pill. I was very lucky that this agreed with my body and I didn't notice any negative side effects except that my periods eventually stopped. Even before I was on the Pill my periods were quite irregular because of my ulcerative colitis, but I asked my doctors about this and they said it was a perfectly normal side effect, which was reassuring. Although for the first two years I was on it, every time I went to get another prescription I always asked again to make sure.

After seven years of being on the same pill, no periods, no problems, I decided to come off it and document the process on my YouTube channel in a series called The Hormone Diaries. Why did you come off the pill?! You had no periods! That's such a blessing! Are you crazy?! I hear you say. Well, yes, maybe I am crazy. But something had shifted in me. I felt numb. I didn't feel like a 'woman'. I didn't experience a cycle, the ups and downs, the mood changes, the body changes, the libido changes. Everything was static and flat and I just wanted to feel my body doing its natural thing. So I decided to stop using hormonal contraception. Six and half weeks later I had my first period in seven years. And it was such a weird experience. But here's the thing, what I've learned from this is that what is right for one person may not be right for you. And what was right for you at one time may not be right for you now. Listen to your body, be kind to it, listen to your lifestyle needs and see what works for you. For now, I'm just going to stick with using condoms, but you never know, that might change in the future after I'm sick of having periods again, or I enter a long-term relationship, or (way into the future) I want to get pregnant. Contraception isn't a 'one-size-fits-all' kind of thing. We're all working it out and we're all trying our best. The main piece of advice that I want to share is another lesson learned from The Hormone Diaries: talk to other people about their experiences. Your experience is valuable information and we shouldn't be shy and keep these things to ourselves. Sharing is caring. I've learned so much from people sharing their experiences with hormones, contraception and periods in the comments on my videos and it has been so helpful to me making my own decisions about my body and my periods.

Chapter 11

STIs

When I was 14, we had a sex education class about STIs which basically consisted of a slideshow presentation of pictures of different genitals with untreated STIs.

This scarred me for life. It made me feel terrified of sex, confused why anyone wouldn't use a condom, and grossed out by everything. This is what I would call sex-negative education; all we were taught was that STIs are horrible and you should fear them, so wear a condom and get tested. The last two bits of advice are good – yes, use condoms and yes, go get tested. But the stigma around STIs that it reinforced did not help. For years I thought that people who had STIs were disgusting and I would shame them to myself and to friends for being dirty and stupid enough to catch one in the first place. Oh how wrong I was. We should be taught to understand STIs, not fear them. And to have compassion for people who do catch them (the statistics say that quite a few of your friends will in your lifetimes) instead of shaming them. We should also be taught how to talk about STIs, especially with sexual partners, because that is a crucial conversation to have in any healthy relationship. STIs can be transmitted through unprotected sexual activity and condoms are the only form of contraception that can protect against pregnancy and STIs, so even if you're on the pill or have the implant, use a condom. We shouldn't create fear around STIs but it is still important to be aware of them, so here's a list of some of the most common:

Chlamydia

The most common STI among young people. Often there are no symptoms, but if left untreated it can cause fertility problems in men and women. Symptoms can include unusual discharge and pain when peeing. It can be transmitted through unprotected vaginal, anal and oral sex, sharing toys and genital-to-genital contact. It can be treated easily with antibiotics.

Gonorrhoea

A bacterial infection, similar to chlamydia. Again, some people don't experience any symptoms, so if you've had unprotected sex, it's best to get checked out. It can be treated with antibiotics; however, there has been an increase in cases of a drug-resistant strand of super-gonorrhoea.

HIV (Human Immunodeficiency Virus)

A virus which attacks the immune system and can develop into AIDS (Acquired Immune Deficiency Syndrome), which is when your body can no longer fight against life-threatening infections. Unlike 30 years ago, an HIV positive result is no longer a death sentence. It is not curable but it is treatable, for most people an early diagnosis can prevent HIV from developing into AIDS. There is now medication that can make the HIV undetectable, so even if you are positive you won't be able to transmit the virus to someone else. HIV can be transmitted through blood, semen or vaginal fluids. So use a condom and if you think you're at risk, get tested.

Genital Herpes

A viral infection that causes sores and blisters around the genitals; it is from the same strand of virus that causes cold sores around the mouth. It is highly contagious and can be passed on through any kind of sexual contact. People with the virus may not experience any symptoms but can still pass it on ... especially immediately before, during and after an outbreak. Because it is a viral infection there is no cure, but there are treatments that can help manage the outbreaks and reduce the risk of passing it on to someone else.

Genital Warts

Caused by HPV (the human papillomavirus), genital warts are the second most common STI amongst young people. They are small growths or bumps on the genital area. Not everyone with HPV will develop genital warts, and it's a different virus that causes warts on the hands or feet. Genital warts are spread by skin-to-skin contact and can be passed on even if they are not visible. You can protect yourself by using condoms but HPV can still be passed on by skin-to-skin contact of the area surrounding the genitals. Treatment for genital warts can be a cream, a lotion or removal by freezing or heating.

Syphilis

It isn't very common, but syphilis is on the rise. It's a bacterial infection that develops in three stages and if left untreated can cause serious illnesses and even death. The first symptom is a painless sore in the genital or anal area and can progress to a rash, small skin growths, flu symptoms, swollen glands, weight loss and patchy hair loss. If caught early, syphilis can be treated with an antibiotic injection.

There are other STIs, not just the ones mentioned here, but these are some of the most common ones. Make sure you use a condom every time you have sex and if you do have unprotected sex, then go get tested as soon as possible. It's always wise to know your status.

Myth-busting

You can get STIs from kissing, hugging, sharing towels, swimming pools or toilet seats.

You can't get most STIs from these things because they are passed on through blood, semen, vaginal fluid or genital contact. But herpes can be transferred through kissing if you have a cold sore and pubic lice can be passed on by sharing towels or bed linen.

You can't get an STI if there's no penetration/ejaculation

Some STIs are passed on through genital contact and they can also be transferred through pre-cum.

HIV only affects men who have sex with men

This comes from the AIDS epidemic in the 1980s which did primarily affect gay and bisexual men. Anal sex is the highest-risk sexual activity for contracting HIV which is why gay men are most at risk, but women and straight men can also get HIV. The virus is carried in semen, vaginal fluid and blood.

You can't get STIs from oral sex

Yes you can. A lot of STIs you can also get from oral sex so to protect yourself make sure you use a condom to cover the penis or a dental dam (a square piece of latex) to cover the vagina or anus.

Only sexually promiscuous people get STIs

No, no, no. Anyone can get an STI and it doesn't matter how many people you have slept with. If you've had unprotected sex, then you're at risk. This is just another myth that shames people who have a lot of sex.

If you have an STI then you can never have sex again

Not true! You can still have sex if you've had an STI in the past, or if you currently have one. Always use a condom and make sure you are open with your sexual partner about it so you take the necessary precautions.

How to talk to your partner about STIs

I'll be honest; I recently had an STI scare. I always use condoms and I've had the odd STI test but not as regularly as I would like to. My genuine advice is (and I will start taking my own advice here, I promise) if you are sexually active and sleeping with different people then get checked out every six months to a year, or every time you change sexual partner. Also, if you are having casual sex then make sure you swap contact details with the other person – it doesn't matter if you plan on texting them or seeing them again. It's a way to get in touch to inform the other person just in case one of you finds out you have an STI. It's not an ideal situation if you find out you have an STI, but you can't tell a recent sexual partner to make sure they also get checked out if you don't have their phone number or full name to look up on Facebook. They might also have it, not get checked out and then unknowingly pass it on to someone else. You would want to know if someone you'd slept with has an STI, right? So this brings us to my story. The other day I had the following conversation with someone I'd slept with two months prior.

Let's call him Matt.

Matt: Hey Hannah
Have you had a sexual health check up recently?

Me: A couple months ago. All clean. Why?
Do you have something? Actually just checked.
It was November last time I got tested

Matt: So, I got checked today. And I was given chlamydia by someone in the past few months. We had protected sex, so it wasn't you

Me: Aaah balls. Cheers for telling me!
I'll get checked up asap. That's one of the good ones though! Take a few pills and it's gone :)

Matt: But I thought I'd let you know, just get checked maybe Yeah :)

Me: Yeah thanks! :D

Matt: Haha no worries, sorry that you might have it. I feel bad as f**k

Me: We used a condom so hopefully not!
But no worries. I don't blame you or anything

Matt: Thank you :) that makes me feel much better

This was the first time I'd ever had this conversation with a sexual partner before but I'm really proud of how we handled it. I'm sure there are other versions of this that don't go down so well. The only things I regret saying are I'm 'all clean' and that chlamydia is 'one of the good ones.' There's no such thing as a 'good' or 'bad' STI. Chlamydia is just one that is easily treatable and I think I wanted him to feel better. And using words like 'clean' to say you don't have any STIs implies that people who do are 'dirty', so I won't be using that language again.

Anyway, spoiler alert: I don't have chlamydia. Condoms really do work guys.

Having the conversation about STIs is important for any sexual relationship – you can even go to the clinic together! My boyfriend and I went to get tested together when we were 17. I'm so glad I had someone to go with because the first time doing something like that can be nerve-wracking. It's also a sign that you really trust, respect and care about the other person and your relationship with them.

What if your partner refuses to get tested and uses the 'don't you trust me?' line? DUMP THEM. OK, maybe not straightaway but you need to ask what the real reason is behind them not wanting to get checked up. Are they convinced that they don't have anything because they've always used protection? Do they think it's embarrassing to go to a sexual health clinic? Do they think they're fine just because they don't have any symptoms? Try and talk to them one on one privately and calmly about it and maybe even hand them this book to read ;). In all seriousness though, if you ask a sexual partner to get tested and they say no, that's a red flag. Going to get tested shows that you care about and have respect for the person you're sleeping with. If a civil conversation doesn't work either, break up with them. Or you could just withhold sex until they get tested.

What it's like getting tested

*T*his is what happens if you go to an NHS-run sexual health clinic in Britain. First of all, Google your nearest one and check if you can make an appointment. Usually if you're just going for a check-up you can use the walk-in clinic, so find out when it is open and get there as early as possible. The later in the day you wait, the busier it gets and walk-ins are first-come first-served.

Depending on whether you go to an old-school clinic or one of the trendy ones (yes, trendy sexual health clinics do exist, e.g. 56 Dean Street in the heart of Soho, London), when you go in you'll either fill out a paper form or an electronic form. I remember walking past the sexual health clinic on Dean Street with my mum on a Saturday afternoon and there was a huge queue of young people spilling out on to the street waiting to get an STI test. I felt so proud. Hell yeah, it is cool to look after your sexual health.

On the form they'll ask your age, gender, whether or not you have any known STIs, what gender/s the people you have sex with are, how many recent sexual partners you've had, if any of them have been a gay or bisexual man. I had actually been seeing a bi guy at the time and the nurse asked me all of these questions about his sex life before me, which I did not know the answers to. Once you've filled out the form about your sordid sexual past, you wait. And then you get called in by a nurse who will have some follow-up questions, and if you're having an HIV and syphilis screening they'll do a blood test. When you're in the room with the nurse, this is the time to ask all the questions you have about sexual and genital health. Do not be embarrassed – they've heard it all. I'll be honest and say I asked if you could transmit chlamydia orally (I didn't know! The answer is yes, yes you can). Once that is done you will privately do your swab – vaginal, anal or oral, or all three. For that, you get total privacy and you can take your time.

Times have changed since the first time I had an STI check-up, when I was 17. For that I lay back in the doctor's chair with my legs in stirrups, they clamped open my vagina and took the swab themselves. I am very pleased at how the system has evolved. All of your details are on the blood test and swab and so later that day you'll get a text telling you your result. If it says 'negative' that means you don't have anything (I know, confusing right?) If it says 'positive' it will tell you what you're positive with and then you can book an appointment to talk about your options and start treatment. The whole process really is fine. It's not scary (unless you're afraid of needles), everyone makes you feel calm and no one makes you feel embarrassed or ashamed. It is really quick (if you get there early so there's no wait) and there is never any harm in going for a check-up. It's always good to know your sexual health status and most STIs are better treated the sooner you find out, so better safe than sorry.

If you do have an STI ... First of all, you are not dirty, gross or disgusting. Secondly, go to your doctor and talk about what you do next. For some STIs you just take a bunch of pills and in a week you're fine. For others it's more complicated than that but you'll be fine. Having an STI is not the end of the world or of your sex life. People live with them and manage them every day and we need to break down the stigma by talking about them more and not shunning or shaming people who have them.

Anonymous on *Chlamydia*

I don't think any of us ever expect to ACTUALLY catch an STI. I never felt like I'd become part of a chlamydia statistic and I never anticipated how having one of the most frequently diagnosed sexually transmitted infections in the world would make me feel.

I've always been the girl with the boyfriend. The girl who never uses condoms because she's in a long-term, trusting, monogamous relationship. During university many of my friends would update me over lunch about their sexual health and though I'd express my concern, my insides would turn … inside out. I've always felt squeamish thinking about sickness and infection and disease. So the idea that these things could be transferred via bodily fluids really REALLY grossed me out. After my partner and I broke up, I mourned the loss of the 'completely 100 per cent actual safe sex' feeling. I nervously began to experiment with different sexual partners. And I quickly re-discovered how much I despise condoms, how much they detract from my feelings of intimacy and arousal, so, a couple of times I asked new lovers if we could rely solely on my contraceptive pill for protection. (Mind you, I was thinking purely about avoiding pregnancy and not at all about picking up any unwanted infections … I was consumed by the 'but it'll never happen to ME' attitude.) In the end, though, we'd never go condom-less without getting joint STI tests. Then I started dating a really attractive, funny guy and fell head-over-heels in love. Or lust. Who cares, he was so hot. Lovust. Let's go with that. And when we decided to make a go of it and move in together, we had THE CHAT.

That conversation consenting couples should have regarding STI test results. I popped into the doctor's office, had a swab test and a blood sample taken. I was 'clean'. I showed him the results and he gave me a very (at the time) reassuring 'oh yeah, me too, my results are at home … we're all good to go!' I believed him. No more questions asked. Because I'm an idiot. Plenty of sexy times commenced. It was all great, up until I discovered he'd been cheating on me. I confronted the other woman and she admitted that they hadn't used condoms – he'd lied to her about me, so now we were both freaking out. 'If he's lied to both of us, who else has he possibly been sleeping with?' It's safe to say, that was the end of that. I bolted.

Fast-forward two weeks of 'please forgive me' texts and anxiety and stress. I'm nervously waiting on new STI results. 'You have chlamydia', the doctor tells me over the phone. 'It's very common and can be caught by having unprotected vaginal, anal or oral sex with someone who's already infected. You're catching it early so you'll be fine, it's treatable, but you're lucky, as it's a silent disease that mostly shows no symptoms. If left untreated, chlamydia can lead to infertility. You'll need to take a single dose of four tablets in one go, and that's it. Be sure to inform anyone you've slept with in recent months.' I felt empty. Disgusted. I couldn't even think straight, or stand up. The words 'common' and 'treatable' did absolutely nothing to lighten the blow. I'd caught an STI that could have left me unable to have children (something I've always wanted) and it was my own fault for blindly trusting a new squeeze. For not demanding to see his test results. I sacrificed my own health for the slightly heightened pleasure of going at it without a condom. The next day I went to get the four tablets needed to treat the chlamydia and swallowed them with a big gulp of water in my kitchen. I'm not sure what I expected ... that instantly I'd be back to normal. That I'd feel clean and sexy and up for it again. But unfortunately that wasn't my experience. I spoke to friends about this at length for a solid month or two afterwards, and it was difficult to describe but I basically felt ... unclean. Dirty. Damaged. Rotten. Disgusting. Maybe it's socialisation, or my innate fear of anything going wrong with my body, or a combination of both, but the experience of catching an STI affected me so much more than I could have anticipated.

I started wearing baggier clothing and doing something I'd never done before – avoiding sex. The first thing a partner will discover about me is that I'm not one of those 'sorry not tonight, I've got a headache' kind of people – I've always had a tremendously high sex drive. Post-STI, I'd go to work events and wild parties and be surrounded by young, attractive, flirtatious people and I'd ... slip off back to my room, alone. It took a lot for me to even allow another person to touch me down there again, and I'm still to this day coming to terms with having anyone go down on me. EVEN THOUGH IT'S GONE. Even though I'm fine, I'm no longer infected, it has left a mental scar. It's constantly in the back of my mind during sexual encounters. I'm going to work hard to shift that, but all of this was avoidable. That's what really gets me.

If I could go back in time and force that test-results conversation to be properly finished, I would. Or I'd simply just wrap his willy. If you're reading this, know that your body seriously is a temple. It's not worth chancing it. Get regular check-ups, be safe and don't risk becoming infertile (or worse) for a fleeting thrill. Nobody and nothing is worth risking your sexual and mental health.

Chapter 12

sexting

When I was a teenager the closest you could get to 'sexting' was phone sex on your pay-as-you-go Nokia 3210 that your parents still paid for, or txts dat looked lyk dis cos u ddnt have enuf credit, or sending really pixelated photos through MSN if you were lucky enough to have a webcam. Now that we are fully in the digital age, and everyone and their mum has a smartphone, the sexting game is a bit different. There's still good old-fashioned phone sex but now you also have Skype sex, there's Snapchat for pictures you want to vanish (beware screenshots), and there are a million ways for you to send photos and videos, and to digitally sexually express yourself.

Why people sext

Personally I'm a big fan of sexting, and although I've shared a lot of personal information in this book I won't be sharing any messages with you. I don't want you stealing my moves. There is nothing wrong with sexting, it's completely up to you and your partner how you communicate and express yourselves sexually. Just test the water and make sure everyone is on the same page first before sending explicit images. No one wants an unsolicited dick pic. But if everyone is consenting and completely up for it then you do you (although if you're sending images or videos then make sure everyone is over 18, in accordance with the law). So why might people want to sext?

Flirting

Sexual expression

Teasing

Alternative to physical sex in long-distance relationships

To get aroused

To communicate what you like more easily than face-to-face

To get yourself off, or someone else off, or both

To play out fantasies/role play

It's easy to stop if you want to

To boost self-esteem (you don't have to send the photos to anyone, they could be just for yourself)

Sexting can be a great way to get to know someone's sexual mind and it can enhance relationships if you don't see your partner that often. Having trust and good communication can make sexting a really fun thing to do, it's just important to make sure everyone is comfortable with it, and can stop it at any point.

Downsides of sexting

Unless you're living under a rock, you will have seen in the news various celebrities having their accounts hacked and nude pictures leaked to the press. Of course this is awful but it is not the fault of the people who are in the photos. What we do privately is our own business and if we want to take sexy naked pictures then we should be able to do that without the fear of them getting into the wrong hands or being shamed for it. But this has created apprehension and fear amongst a lot of people. And even though you are not at fault at all if you and your partner want to sext or you want to take saucy pictures of yourself, there are still some risks that you should consider.

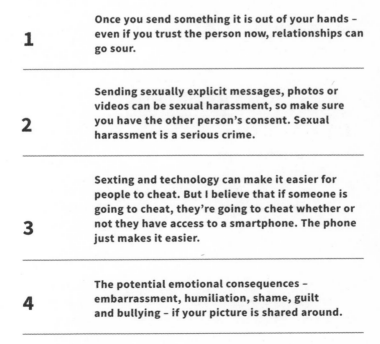

1 Once you send something it is out of your hands – even if you trust the person now, relationships can go sour.

2 Sending sexually explicit messages, photos or videos can be sexual harassment, so make sure you have the other person's consent. Sexual harassment is a serious crime.

3 Sexting and technology can make it easier for people to cheat. But I believe that if someone is going to cheat, they're going to cheat whether or not they have access to a smartphone. The phone just makes it easier.

4 The potential emotional consequences – embarrassment, humiliation, shame, guilt and bullying – if your picture is shared around.

No one deserves to have their private pictures shared without their consent and no one is 'asking for it' by simply taking the pictures in the first place. But you must be aware of the risks and then make your own informed decision. And by no means think that you have to because other people are doing it, or because someone asked nicely. Don't feel pressured to do something you don't want to do and vice versa, don't pressure people into sexting. It's not for everyone.

The Law and Sexting

Sexual harassment – sending unsolicited sexual messages, photos or videos or harassing someone to send some to you.
Revenge porn – the publication of explicit messages, photos or videos of someone who has not consented to them being shared.
Blackmail – using explicit messages, images or videos to coerce someone into sexual acts or staying in a relationship with you.

DON'T DO

THESE THINGS

They are illegal.

The law also states that sexting is illegal for those under the age of 18, but this is slightly more complicated. So here's Kate Parker on what the law says about sexting.

Kate Parker:

A lot of media coverage of 'sexting' law makes it sound as though it's a new piece of legislation. It's not. 'Sexting' is governed by section 1 of the Protection of Children Act 1978 which, as its title suggests, has been around for almost 40 years. It was originally enacted to crack down on the spread of child pornography, but it has been resuscitated to deal with the modern phenomenon of 'sexting'. It has already faced a lot of criticism from lawyers for being too harsh to deal with what is, essentially, young people sending explicit images of themselves over text. So, what does section 1 actually say?

'It is an offence for a person

a) to take, or permit to be taken or to make, any indecent photograph or pseudo-photograph of a child; or

b) to distribute or show such indecent photographs or pseudo-photographs; or

c) to have in his possession such indecent photographs or pseudo-photographs with a view to their being distributed or shown by himself or others'.

A few notes before we get going. Firstly, ignore if you can the law's exclusive reference to the male gender. This law of course applies to everyone, but such subtle linguistic equality is clearly too much to expect from Parliament.

A 'pseudo-photograph' includes images which have been digitally constructed on computers to look like real photographs, and a 'child' is anyone under the age of 18. 'Indecent' is interpreted subjectively but you can probably imagine the sort of thing it covers: naked images of someone's breast/bum/groin area.

As you'll have realised from the number of verbs in that one extract, this law criminalises a wide variety of acts. Anyone who takes, shows or possesses (with a view to showing another) an indecent image of someone under 18 years old could fall foul of this law, even if that image was taken consensually and even if that image was a selfie.

Picture a scenario in which, in a loving relationship with my boyfriend, I let him take photographs of me whilst naked.
I'm 17 (which, as you'll know, is over the legal age of consent). I could be prosecuted

for permitting such photos to be taken. My boyfriend could be prosecuted for taking those photos and for having them on his mobile phone ('possessing' them), with the intention of showing them to me.

Picture another scenario in which, as a treat for my boyfriend (or, hey, because I think my boobs are just looking great one day), I decide to take a topless photo of myself on my mobile phone. I'm still 17. Again, I could be prosecuted on the basis that I took those images and had them on my mobile phone with the intention of showing them to my boyfriend.

There is a further law, section 160 of the Criminal Justice Act 1988, that criminalises those who possess photos even without the intent to show them to another. However, it is a defence under this law to say that you hadn't seen the photographs yourself and had no reason to suspect they were indecent (covering, for example, spam email that might go straight through to your junk mail folder), or that you received the photograph without requesting it and you did not keep it for an unreasonable length of time. It will fall to the court to determine what an 'unreasonable' length of time is. If you've ever received an explicit image of someone

under 18 without requesting it, you'd have to delete it pretty quickly to avoid a prosecution. You can probably now see why the law around 'sexting' is far from ideal: it seems strange to be criminalising consensual, willing acts, just because the subject happens to be young. And the sanctions are steep. Under section 1 of the Protection of Children Act, the maximum sentence is 10 years' imprisonment. Under section 160 of the Criminal Justice Act 1988, the maximum sentence is five years' imprisonment. But it's important to remember that every prosecution has to pass a two-stage test. The Crown Prosecution Service (the body that prosecutes on behalf of the state) has to ask itself, is there sufficient evidence for a realistic prospect of conviction?

Secondly, is it in the public interest to bring this prosecution? The CPS may take the view that it's not really in the public interest to prosecute a 17-year-old for the sending of a few explicit images. It must be remembered that the law is originally intended to combat paedophilia. Even if a prosecution does follow, teenagers convicted of 'sexting' won't face the maximum sentence. For young people, the court may choose to impose a fine, or something called a Referral Order or a Youth Rehabilitation Order is likely: a form of punishment that is dealt with in the community. It may even be that the police choose to deal with such behaviour by way of a caution, which doesn't involve coming to court at all. Whilst this is a very low-level punishment, it's important to remember that it could still limit travel and employment opportunities in later life. Probably not worth it for a few pics of your boobs.

A final word of caution: 'sexting' is something that is very difficult to undo. Once that picture is out there, it is extremely difficult to claw back. It may be that, in a trusting relationship, you can be certain that image won't be seen by anyone other than the two of you. But what happens if that relationship ends on bad terms? What happens if someone else gets hold of your mobile phone, or the phone of your partner? Quite apart from the legal repercussions discussed above, such an experience can be incredibly damaging and difficult to deal with. Obviously, in that situation, it's the fault of whoever has spread that image without your consent. But think very carefully before putting the content out, because from that point onwards it is (quite literally) out of your hands.

Chapter 13

sex shaming

284

You're a slut

I f I had 10p for every time I've been called a slut, either in real life or online, then I could buy myself a luxury sex toy. To be honest, making videos talking about sex on the Internet doesn't really help my cause but if talking openly about sex and educating people is the definition of a slut then hell yes I'm a slut! However, here's the thing, there is no real definition of a slut. When I made my video 'Do I Look Like A Slut?', I asked people, 'what is a slut?' and the main definitions were:

A woman who has a lot of sex

A woman who dresses in revealing clothing

A woman who teases and flirts but doesn't sleep with you

A woman who lies and cheats

So let's talk about these ...

A woman who has a lot of sex

Can someone please tell me the number of sexual partners where you tip over the edge from 'experienced' to 'slut'? Because no one's told me the official figure, so I'm confused. Also, a friendly reminder that people in relationships are generally having a lot more sex than single people who are having casual sex here and there. And having casual sex is fine. As long as it's consensual and it's coming from a positive place of pleasure, curiosity, connection, trust and respect, then there's nothing wrong with what you're doing.

A woman who dresses in revealing clothing

There's no correlation between how you dress and your sexual behaviour. There are a lot of reasons why someone might dress a certain way – it's a form of self-expression. If you see a woman on a night out and she's got high heels, a short skirt and a cleavage-heavy top on, there's that voice in your head and I'm ashamed to admit I get it too. That voice says, 'Oh wow, she looks like a bit of a slut'. Some people's head voices even say that out loud. But stop. As soon as you think it, stop yourself and check yourself. Women can wear whatever they want, it's not an invitation and it's not sending out any messages other than 'this is what I chose to wear today'.

A woman who teases and flirts but doesn't sleep with you

This one is my favourite. The double standard is just too perfect. If you presume I sleep with a lot of people, I'm a slut. If I don't want to have sex with you, I'm still a slut. Amazing. Here's a shocking idea: a woman can sleep with a whole bunch of different people and not you, she can sleep with a whole bunch of people and you, she can sleep with only you, she can sleep with no one at all, and none of those scenarios make her a 'slut'.

A woman who lies and cheats

This woman is still not a slut. A woman who lies and cheats, or anyone who lies and cheats, is maybe just a bit of a mean, manipulative person or is perhaps going through some stuff. If someone cheats on you that doesn't make them a slut, although it doesn't make them the most ideal partner either. But calling someone a slut because of bad behaviour in a relationship isn't going to solve any of the real issues. So either break up with them or talk to them properly about what's going on.

You may have noticed a pattern, which is that in all of these examples, no one is actually a 'slut' and that's because sluts don't exist. It's a word used to control (mostly) women's sexual behaviour. I remember as a teenager, a 'slut' or a 'slag' (because I'm from the north) was one of the worst things you could be called. So us girls behaved a certain way or made it seem like we behaved a certain way; when we got dressed to go out we'd ask, 'do I look like a slut?' desperately making sure that we didn't. Maybe it stopped us from pursuing what we wanted or talking openly about things we wanted to discuss; and worst of all, it turned us against each other. I have a lot of regret and sadness when I think about how I used to judge other women and my thoughts now are summed up very nicely by Tina Fey's character in *Mean Girls*: 'You all have to stop calling each other sluts and whores. It just makes it ok for guys to call you sluts and whores.' Oh Ms Norbury, so wise.

There's also a gross double standard with the word 'slut'.

I've mainly been talking about women and that's because slut is inherently a gendered word. You can't call a dude a slut. If you do you have to put the prefix of 'man' before it so he'd be a 'man-slut'. The double standard isn't just in the language but in the types of sexual behaviour we reward and punish depending on your gender. If a woman has a lot of sex with men then she's a slut, if a man has a lot of sex with women then he's a hero/player/legend/stud – all positive things in our society. In school I remember someone telling me that people always lie about the number of sexual partners they've had – men always add three to the real number and women always subtract three. Again, these harmful double standards were playing out in my life when I was really young. I remember thinking, 'does this mean I should tell people I've slept with minus three people? Because that's stupid.' Having sex doesn't make you a slut or a stud. It's just sex. It's your body, your choices, your behaviour and your personal relationship with the other person. Lots of casual sex may feel right to one person but to another it's just not for them. It's about how you feel. Are you happy with your sex life? Yes, maybe having too much sex is a problem if you're doing it for the wrong reasons and it's making you unhappy. But that's a completely personal thing and still doesn't make you a slut. Your sex life is your sex life and it's up to you how you write that story.

You're a prude

On the other side of the coin, there are people who are shamed for not having enough sex. Society is weird with its double standards.

YOU'RE HAVING <u>TOO MUCH</u> SEX YOU'RE A SLUT,

YOU'RE <u>NOT HAVING ENOUGH</u> SEX YOU'RE A PRUDE VIRGIN!

You can't win. Despite the fact that healthy relationships, LGBQT+ issues, sexual pleasure and STIs aren't talked about enough, sex is still everywhere. It's in our films, on TV, in music videos, advertising, video games, etc. Our whole culture is sexualised yet we're missing basic sex and relationship education. In a heavily sexualised society, where it feels like everyone is having sex, people at school ask questions like, 'how far have you gone?' and when you get to university everyone seems to be having sex with each other, you might feel like you're not doing something right if you're not having, or don't want to have, these same experiences.

We seem to have gone in the other direction when it comes to sex shaming. If you're not really interested in having casual sex, you only want to sleep with people who you're in a loving relationship with and you have a low number of sexual partners then some people might shame you for that. We've been sexually 'liberated' now and so some people think that sexual freedom is synonymous with having loads of sex all the time with lots of different people, but that's not the case. You can also choose not to have sex with people and it's still liberating if you've chosen it. So you're not a prude. What is a prude anyway? To me it seems like a word that's used to make people feel bad about not being sexual in the way that society expects. Or it's used by people who feel sore about being rejected.

There is no right or wrong kind of sex life, there's just whatever works for you. There's no hierarchy in sex – who's doing it right, enough, with the right people. But no one is in a position to pass judgement on anyone's sexual preferences, sexual behaviour, the way they dress, how they look, etc.

It's really none of our business.

You're a freak

We also like to shame things that we don't understand, and one of those is the kinkier side to sex. Everyone has different preferences, desires and unique sexualities and so it's no surprise that there's a whole range of sexual practices, fetishes and what-not to explore. There's a meme that states the rules of the Internet, and Rule No. 34 is that 'if it exists, there's porn for it – no exceptions.' And it's probably right. There is someone out there amongst the seven billion people on this planet who enjoys jaffa cake porn or gets off on that sound of nails on a chalkboard. We can't control what we're into, and trying out new things with partners can be fun and exciting. Yes, it's not for everyone but that doesn't mean those who do enjoy a bit of BDSM (Bondage, Discipline/Dominance, Submission/Sadomasochism) or role-play should be judged. The most important thing is that everything is consensual, there's trust and respect, and you have safe-words and aftercare. A lot of kinks or fetishes don't get represented in society in a positive, healthy way. Even a foot fetish, which is the most common fetish, is most often referred to in jokes or in disgust.

So whatever someone's sexual peculiarities, especially if they're different to your own – let's be kind to each other. No one wins in this game of sex shaming, it just makes people feel awful about themselves, and confused and lonely. How about some sex praising?

Hey, so you had a one-night stand last night and you're super-happy about it and now you're just going to go about your life? Cool! Go you! Have a great day!

Oh you're into peeing on people and your partner is totally fine with that and you have a really loving and healthy relationship and sex life. Congratulations!

You've not had sex in two years because you've not met anyone who you want to do that with and you're having a blast spending time on your work, friends and hobbies? Of course there's nothing wrong with you. You're great! Have a nice life! You don't want to tell me all the intimate details of your sex life? That's fine! I won't tell you mine if it makes you feel uncomfortable. Now let's bake a cake.

Wouldn't that be nice?

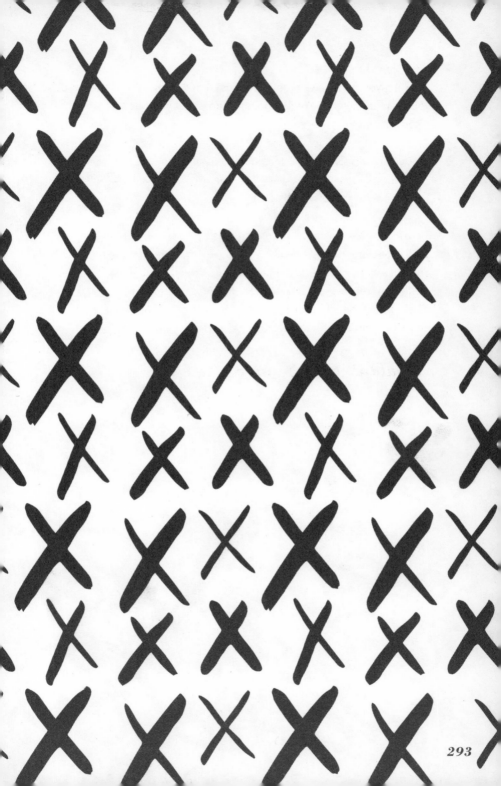

293

e you so

please

ou like it o

miss you

you to th

and back

to me mou

nk about ye

yday pleas

me you got

chocolates

Done it

conclusion

Now I'm sure you're all wondering, 'Hannah, what happened with that guy? Are you OK?' If you recall, whilst writing this book, I got dumped. At the point of writing this it has been almost two months since said dumping occurred.

And by the time you are reading this it will have been even longer. Relationships and dating don't always have that perfect narrative arc like they do in the movies. In real life, nothing happens in an order that makes sense and sometimes there's no end or conclusion to things. Right now I'm fine. I'm over him. I'm not crying over him anymore. And even though he pops into my head every now and then there's no sadness or anger that comes along with that. It's more of a, 'hmm I wonder what he's up to now?' kind of thing. But that being said, I actually haven't seen him since it happened. I say I'm fine but I'm also waiting for that moment when we bump into each other at a party or something and suddenly I'm confronted with all the feelings that I thought I'd already dealt with. But that hasn't happened yet, so for the sake of a satisfying narrative and a happy ending: I'm fine. I'm happy and single again.

(Update! Our mutual friends are hosting a Halloween party and I saw that he clicked attending on Facebook so brb as I find the best possible costume ever so I look really cool and attractive and I'll have a great time and he'll be all like 'damn I'm an idiot for letting her go'. Or not, we'll see.)

(Update! Update! So I went to the Halloween party as Eleven from Stranger Things *and I looked amazing but he hadn't seen the show (!?) so it was wasted on him. You know how I said if I saw him again I might be suddenly confronted with all the feelings? Well, yeah that happened. I'll spare you the details but it basically ended with us kissing and crying together and his face paint had transferred onto my face. Despite what you might think I actually got a lot of closure that night. We haven't seen each other since but texted as friends and it feels good.)*

What I'm trying to say is that the world of sex, dating, relationships, love, self-discovery and acceptance isn't always easy. Doing it is hard and no one is perfect at it. There isn't a single person or a person in a relationship that I know (myself included) that has completely got it together. Sex and relationships education isn't just something you learn and experience and then you're done. It's a process that takes your whole life and this is the accumulation of my knowledge and experience up until now. I hope that reading this book has had a positive impact on your journey wherever you're at in it. One of the things I hope you've got from this book is that everyone is different. Maybe it's hard for you to relate to me because I'm so open about sex that I'm writing a bloody book about it. But if you're less experienced, a little more quiet about the subject, a bit more conservative about all things sex, then that's fine, too. I was at a party recently and I sat down on the sofa next to an acquaintance.

We were talking and out of the blue she said to me that she's sorry if she's ever seemed distant or cold around me but it's because she feels intimidated by me. I was kind of shocked. Firstly, because how could she be intimidated by me? I thought she was wonderful and I'm kind of in awe of everything she does, and because she just told me. She opened up and said something to me that was probably quite hard to admit. And I thought that was really cool. I asked her why and she said it was because of my openness about sex. She respected what I was doing but we had different opinions about how to lead our personal sex lives and she was afraid that I would judge her for her choices. I thought this was completely ridiculous. But this is what happens when you don't talk or open up to the people in your life. You assume they think one way or you expect them to behave in a certain way but you're only going to find out by talking. Communication is one of the most important things in any kind of healthy relationship and in life in general. I explained to her that I had lived with girls at university who had the same beliefs and made the same choices as her that were different to mine, but we didn't judge each other. There was mutual respect that recognised that what was right for one person may not be right for another. We didn't impose our views on each other and there was compassion and curiosity for each others' lives. She seemed reassured by this and so now we understand each other better.

Sex and relationships education is important to me because it is so fundamental to how we live our lives, how we feel about ourselves and how we interact with one another. And not passing any judgement on other people's bodies, identities, behaviours or choices is part of that education. Learning about this stuff from a young age can help a lot of people feel less alone, help them feel normal and in control of their bodies and their future. It can give them the tools to make the best decisions for themselves and know what to do when things don't go to plan. It can make you feel comfortable in your skin and be proud of who are you. On a more practical level, SRE is important for preventing the spread of STIs and avoiding unplanned pregnancies. It strives to make every sexual encounter a consensual one and to stop people from being bullied or isolated because of their gender identity, sexuality or sexual preferences. Sex and relationships education is important. Please spread this message. Please educate your peers. Everyone has the power to be a sex educator in their own community. You don't have to be an expert – I would know because I'm not one either. I'm just obsessed with learning about sex and helping others learn too.

And I'm still learning and the world is still learning and that makes me really excited.

ove you so
uch please
you like it
I miss you
e you to
and b
k to me
hink about
eryday ple
me you g
chocolat

302

resources

Information & Clinics

NHS
http://www.nhs.uk/Livewell/Sexualhealthtopics/Pages/
Sexual-health-hub.aspx

Brook
http://www.brook.org.uk/

Family Planning Association
http://www.fpa.org.uk/

Relationships

Disrespect Nobody
https://www.disrespectnobody.co.uk/

The Mix
http://www.themix.org.uk/
0808 808 4994

ChildLine
https://www.childline.org.uk/
0800 1111

Sexual Violence Support

Rape Crisis
http://rapecrisis.org.uk/

Rape and Sexual Abuse Support Centre
http://www.rasasc.org.uk/
0808 802 9999

LGBTQ+

Stonewall
http://www.stonewall.org.uk/

Switchboard
http://switchboard.lgbt/
0300 330 0630

Terrence Higgins Trust
http://www.tht.org.uk/

Stay Curious

Sexplanations
https://www.youtube.com/user/sexplanations

Sex Education Forum
http://www.sexeducationforum.org.uk/

Sexpression
http://sexpression.org.uk/

Sex Geekdom
http://www.sexgeekdom.com/

index

A

abuse 20, 22, 26, 86, 141 *see also* sexual abuse
abusive relationships 20, 23, 24
abortion 249–251
abstinence 94
acne 241, 245
addiction *see* porn addiction
adult cinema 179, 180
age of consent 64, 122, 132, 278
AIDS 258, 260
alcohol 117, 122, 125–127, 134, 140, 228
allies 109, 110, 111, 112
anal sex 61, 174, 258, 260, 268
androgyny 81, 85, 99
Angus, Thongs and Full-Frontal Snogging 36
antibiotics 258, 259
anuses 137, 189, 261
anxiety 172, 268
apologising 112
asexual people 89, 90, 94–95, 105
asexuality 89, 94–95, 151
ASL *see* sign language

B

bacterial infections 258, 259
Barcelona 175
BDSM 167
'beer goggles' 126
being dumped 39–41, 297
being single 29–35, 39, 298
biological sex (bio-sex) 79
bisexual people 92–93, 260, 265
bisexuality 77, 88, 92–93, 97
blackmail 276
bladders 202
bleeding 62
blood 194, 258, 260
blood tests 266
blowjobs 167, 174

D

E

F

G

H

I

J

K

L

oral sex 61, 167, 258, 261, 268

orgasms 45, 64, 126, 148, 149, 150, 152, 153, 154, 165, 166, 168, 170, 171, 172, 182, 183, 214, 225, 227–231

ovaries 240

ovulation 242, 244

oxytocin 63

P

paedophilia 280

pansexual people 52, 88, 92

pansexuality 52, 88, 92, 97

Parker, Kate 132, 133–141, 277–281

partners 17, 18, 22, 32, 33, 35, 41, 47, 48, 51, 52, 53, 63, 94, 103, 117, 119, 121, 129, 150, 153, 166, 167, 171, 175, 190, 228, 230, 233, 249, 251, 257, 261, 262, 264, 265, 267, 269, 281, 286, 288, 292

'passing' 84

patch (contraceptive) 244–245

penetration/penetrative sex 60, 61, 62, 64, 130, 137, 152, 165, 166, 168, 260

penises 31, 60, 62, 63, 64, 79, 81, 84, 85, 137, 152, 164, 182, 187, 188, 200–203, 216, 228, 240, 244, 246, 261

perineum 189

periods 70, 71, 72, 193–196, 238, 241, 243, 245, 249, 250, 252, 253

pharmacies 249

phones 18, 21, 22, 273, 275, 279, 281

photos 276, 277, 288

PHSE (Personal, Social Health Education) 246

the Pill 71, 72, 238, 240–241, 243, 252, 258

PMDD 195, 196

PMS 194, 195, 196, 241, 245

police 23, 144, 281

polyamory 50, 51–53

porn (pornography) 154, 156, 157, 158, 163–183, 276, 277

    feminist porn 175

    sex-positive porn 175, 176–180

    porn addiction 170–174

possessiveness 21

Poynter, Rikki 128–131

pre-cum 157, 247, 260

pregnancy 64, 237, 250, 251, 258 *see also* getting pregnant

pressure 21, 218, 276

Pretty Woman 24

W

XYZ